FROM A LOGICAL POINT OF VIEW

FROM A LOGICAL
POINT OF VIEW

 *Logico-Philosophical Essays*

Willard Van Orman Quine
Edgar Pierce Professor of Philosophy
Harvard University

Second Edition, revised

HARVARD UNIVERSITY PRESS
Cambridge, Massachusetts
and London, England

LIBRARY OF CONGRESS CATALOG CARD NUMBER 79-92851
ISBN 0-674-32350-5 (CLOTH)
ISBN 0-674-32351-3 (PAPER)

To my
Mother and Father
H. V. Q.—C. R. Q.

FOREWORD, 1980

In 1950, having *Methods of Logic* and a revision of *Mathematical Logic* in hand, I set my sights on a book of more broadly philosophical character. It proved in the fullness of time to be *Word and Object*, and the fullness of time was nine years. I foresaw by 1952 that it would be a long pull and became impatient to make some of my philosophical views conveniently accessible meanwhile. Henry Aiken and I were with our wives in a Greenwich Village nightspot when I told him of the plan, and Harry Belafonte had just sung the calypso "From a logical point of view." Henry noted that this would do nicely as a title for the volume, and so it did.

The book did nicely as well. In the course of its two editions and its many printings it sold nearly forty thousand copies in English and I have no notion how many in Spanish, Italian, Polish, German, and Japanese. Eight of the nine essays have reappeared also independently in one or more anthologies, and each in one or more translations. The first two, indeed, have been anthologized to extinction: twenty-four and twenty-five times respectively and in seven and six languages. I am much gratified and flattered by all this, and likewise by the readiness of my friends at Harvard University Press to take over the paperback rights and keep up the output.

The time for revision is past. The book is dated, and its dates are 1953 and 1961. On the present occasion I have revised just a single page, one that contained mistaken criticism of Church and Smullyan. It is page 154, amid the tumultuous pages where most of the 1961 revision took place.

But I shall improve the opportunity in this preface for a few caveats. One is that "On what there is" is nominalistic neither in doctrine nor in motivation. I was concerned rather with ascribing ontologies than with evaluating them. Moreover, in likening the physicists' posits to the gods of Homer, in that essay and in "Two dogmas," I was talking epistemology and not metaphysics. Posited objects can be real. As I wrote elsewhere, to call a posit a posit is not to patronize it.

The holism in "Two dogmas" has put many readers off, but I think its fault is one of emphasis. All we really need in the way of holism, for the purposes to which it is put in that essay, is to appreciate that empirical content is shared by the statements of science in clusters and cannot for the most part be sorted out among them. Practically the relevant cluster is indeed never the whole of science; there is a grading off, and I recognized it, citing the example of the brick houses on Elm Street.

Both that essay and the next, "The problem of meaning in linguistics," reflected a dim view of the notion of meaning. A discouraging response from somewhat the fringes of philosophy has been that my problem comes of taking words as bare strings of phonemes rather than seeing that they are strings with meaning. Naturally, they say, if I insist on meaningless strings I shall be at a loss for meanings. They fail to see that a bare and identical string of phonemes can *have* a meaning, or several, in one or several languages, through its use by sundry people or peoples, much as I can have accounts in several banks and relatives in several countries without somehow containing them or being several persons. It is usually convenient elsewhere in linguistics to distinguish homomorphs by meanings or history—*sound* (sonus) and *sound* (sanus), for example—but when we are philosophically concerned about meaning we had best not bury it. I hope this paragraph has been superfluous for most readers.

Finally, some technical remarks about "New foundations." We see in pages 98–99 the superiority of ML over NF in respect of mathematical induction and the existence of the class of natural numbers. There remains, however, this related infirmity in ML: Rosser has shown that the class of natural numbers cannot be proved in ML to be a set, or element, if ML is consistent.[1] We can still add an axiom to that effect, and indeed we need it for the theory of real numbers. But it is inelegant to have to add it.

NF and ML can be further criticized for allowing self-membership, which beclouds individuation. The glory of classes, over against properties, is their clear individuation: they are identical if and only if they have the same members. This, however, is relative individuation; classes are individuated only as clearly as their members. Under self-membership the individuation ceases to wind down.

Russell's theory of types has an epistemological advantage over NF and ML: it lends itself to a more plausible reconstruction of the genesis of high-level class concepts.[2] From the theory of types to the set theories of Zermelo and von Neumann, in turn, a natural transition can be made.[3] NF is to be reckoned as an artificial alternative devised afterward for its convenience and elegance; and ML is another. The advantages are real, despite the above reservations.

During the forty-odd years since NF was first published, much ingenious work has been done by Rosser, Beneš, Specker, Orey, Henson, Jensen, Boffa, Grishin, and others in hopes of either deriving a contradiction or proving that the system is consistent if a more classical set theory is consistent. The problem is still open, but a number of curious and surprising relationships have been uncovered in the course of the search.[4]

Cambridge, Massachusetts   *W. V. Q.*

---

[1] J. B. Rosser, "The axiom of Infinity in Quine's New Foundations," *Journal of Symbolic Logic* 17 (1952), 238–242.

[2] See *The Roots of Reference* (La Salle, Ill.: Open Court, 1973), pp. 120ff.

[3] See *Set Theory and Its Logic* (Cambridge: Harvard, 1963, 1969), §§ 38, 43.

[4] See M. Boffa, "On the axiomatization of NF," *Collogues Internationaux du C.N.R.S.*, No. 249 (1975), pp. 157–159, and "The consistency probelm for NF," *Journal of Symbolic Logic* 42 (1977), 215–220, and further references in both papers. See also E. B. Jensen, "On the consistency of a slight modification of Quine's *New Foundations*," in D. Davidson and J. Hintikka, eds., *Words and Objections* (Dordrecht: Reidel, 1969), pp. 278–291.

FOREWORD TO THE SECOND EDITION

The principal revision affects pages 152–159, on the controversial topic of modal logic. A point that was made in those pages underwent radical extension on page 198 of my *Word and Object* (New York, 1960); and lately the situation has further clarified itself, thanks in part to a current doctoral dissertation by my student Dagfinn Føllesdal. These revised pages embody the resulting assessment of the situation.

Independently of that matter, I have made substantive emendations also of pages 103, 118, 125, 148, and 150.

Boston, Mass., April 1961   *W. V. Q.*

PREFACE

Several of these essays have been printed whole in journals; others are in varying degrees new. Two main themes run through them. One is the problem of meaning, particularly as involved in the notion of an analytic statement. The other is the notion of ontological commitment, particularly as involved in the problem of universals.

Various previously published papers which seemed to call for inclusion presented twofold problems. For one thing, they overlapped as papers will which are so written as to spare readers excessive use of libraries. For another, they contained parts which I had grown to recognize as badly formulated or worse. The upshot was that several essays seemed to warrant fairly integral reproduction under their original titles, while others had to be chopped, culled, mixed, eked out with new material, and redivided according to new principles of unification and individuation which brought new titles in their train. For the provenience of what is not new see Origins of the Essays, in the back pages.

The pair of themes named at the top of this page is pursued through the book with the aid, increasingly, of the technical devices of logic. Hence there comes a point, midway, when those themes must be interrupted for the purpose of some elementary technical preparation in logic. "New foundations" is reprinted both for this purpose and for its own sake; for it has figured in subsequent literature, and offprints continue to be sought. Its reproduction here creates an occasion also for supplementary remarks, touching on those subsequent findings and relating the system of "New foundations" to other set theories. However, this intrusion of pure logic has been kept resolutely within bounds.

As noted in some detail in the back pages, the content of this volume is in large part reprinted or adapted from the *Review of Metaphysics*, the *Philosophical Review*, the *Journal of Philosophy*, the *American Mathematical Monthly*, the *Journal of Symbolic Logic*, the *Proceedings of the American Academy of Arts and Sciences*, and *Philosophical Studies*. I am grateful to the editors of these seven periodicals and to the University of Minnesota Press for their kind permission to make this further use of the material.

I am obliged to Professors Rudolf Carnap and Donald Davidson for helpful criticisms of early drafts of "New foundations" and "Two dogmas" respectively, and to Professor Paul Bernays for noting an error in the first printing of "New foundations." The critique of analyticity to which "Two dogmas" is in large part devoted is an outcome of informal discussions, oral and written, in which I have engaged from 1939 onward with Professors Carnap, Alonzo Church, Nelson Goodman, Alfred Tarski, and Morton White; to them I am indebted certainly for stimulation of the essay, and probably for content. To Goodman I am indebted also for criticism of two of the papers from which "Logic and the reification of universals" was in part drawn; and to White for discussion which influenced the present form of that essay.

I thank Mrs. Martin Juhn for her good typing, and the administrators of the Harvard Foundation for a grant in aid. I am grateful to Messrs. Donald P. Quimby and S. Marshall Cohen for able assistance with the index and proofs.

W. V. QUINE

Cambridge, Massachusetts

CONTENTS

FROM A LOGICAL POINT OF VIEW

I

ON WHAT THERE IS

A curious thing about the ontological problem is its simplicity. It can be put in three Anglo-Saxon monosyllables: 'What is there?' It can be answered, moreover, in a word—'Everything'—and everyone will accept this answer as true. However, this is merely to say that there is what there is. There remains room for disagreement over cases; and so the issue has stayed alive down the centuries.

Suppose now that two philosophers, McX and I, differ over ontology. Suppose McX maintains there is something which I maintain there is not. McX can, quite consistently with his own point of view, describe our difference of opinion by saying that I refuse to recognize certain entities. I should protest, of course, that he is wrong in his formulation of our disagreement, for I maintain that there are no entities, of the kind which he alleges, for me to recognize; but my finding him wrong in his formulation of our disagreement is unimportant, for I am committed to considering him wrong in his ontology anyway.

When *I* try to formulate our difference of opinion, on the other hand, I seem to be in a predicament. I cannot admit that there are some things which McX countenances and I do not, for in admitting that there are such things I should be contradicting my own rejection of them.

It would appear, if this reasoning were sound, that in any ontological dispute the proponent of the negative side suffers the disadvantage of not being able to admit that his opponent disagrees with him.

This is the old Platonic riddle of nonbeing. Nonbeing must

1

in some sense be, otherwise what is it that there is not? This tangled doctrine might be nicknamed *Plato's beard;* historically it has proved tough, frequently dulling the edge of Occam's razor.

It is some such line of thought that leads philosophers like McX to impute being where they might otherwise be quite content to recognize that there is nothing. Thus, take Pegasus. If Pegasus *were* not, McX argues, we should not be talking about anything when we use the word; therefore it would be nonsense to say even that Pegasus is not. Thinking to show thus that the denial of Pegasus cannot be coherently maintained, he concludes that Pegasus is.

McX cannot, indeed, quite persuade himself that any region of space-time, near or remote, contains a flying horse of flesh and blood. Pressed for further details on Pegasus, then, he says that Pegasus is an idea in men's minds. Here, however, a confusion begins to be apparent. We may for the sake of argument concede that there is an entity, and even a unique entity (though this is rather implausible), which is the mental Pegasus-idea; but this mental entity is not what people are talking about when they deny Pegasus.

McX never confuses the Parthenon with the Parthenon-idea. The Parthenon is physical; the Parthenon-idea is mental (according anyway to McX's version of ideas, and I have no better to offer). The Parthenon is visible; the Parthenon-idea is invisible. We cannot easily imagine two things more unlike, and less liable to confusion, than the Parthenon and the Parthenon-idea. But when we shift from the Parthenon to Pegasus, the confusion sets in—for no other reason than that McX would sooner be deceived by the crudest and most flagrant counterfeit than grant the nonbeing of Pegasus.

The notion that Pegasus must be, because it would otherwise be nonsense to say even that Pegasus is not, has been seen to lead McX into an elementary confusion. Subtler minds, taking the same precept as their starting point, come out with theories of Pegasus which are less patently misguided than McX's, and correspondingly more difficult to eradicate. One of these subtler minds is named, let us say, Wyman. Pegasus, Wyman maintains, has his being as an unactualized possible. When we say of Pegasus that there is no such thing, we are saying, more precisely, that Pegasus does not have the special attribute of actuality. Saying that Pegasus is not actual is on a par, logically, with saying that the Parthenon is not red; in either case we are saying something about an entity whose being is unquestioned.

Wyman, by the way, is one of those philosophers who have united in ruining the good old word 'exist'. Despite his espousal of unactualized possibles, he limits the word 'existence' to actuality—thus preserving an illusion of ontological agreement between himself and us who repudiate the rest of his bloated universe. We have all been prone to say, in our common-sense usage of 'exist', that Pegasus does not exist, meaning simply that there is no such entity at all. If Pegasus existed he would indeed be in space and time, but only because the word 'Pegasus' has spatio-temporal connotations, and not because 'exists' has spatio-temporal connotations. If spatio-temporal reference is lacking when we affirm the existence of the cube root of 27, this is simply because a cube root is not a spatio-temporal kind of thing, and not because we are being ambiguous in our use of 'exist'.[1] However, Wyman, in an ill-conceived effort to appear agreeable, genially grants us the nonexistence of Pegasus and then, contrary to what *we* meant by nonexistence of Pegasus, insists that Pegasus *is*. Existence is one thing, he says, and subsistence is another. The only way I know of coping with this obfuscation of issues is to *give* Wyman the word 'exist'. I'll try not to use it again; I still have 'is'. So much for lexicography; let's get back to Wyman's ontology.

[1] The impulse to distinguish terminologically between existence as applied to objects actualized somewhere in space-time and existence (or subsistence or being) as applied to other entities arises in part, perhaps, from an idea that the observation of nature is relevant only to questions of existence of the first kind. But this idea is readily refuted by counterinstances such as 'the ratio of the number of centaurs to the number of unicorns'. If there were such a ratio, it would be an abstract entity, viz. a number. Yet it is only by studying nature that we conclude that the number of centaurs and the number of unicorns are both 0 and hence that there is no such ratio.

Wyman's overpopulated universe is in many ways unlovely. It offends the aesthetic sense of us who have a taste for desert landscapes, but this is not the worst of it. Wyman's slum of possibles is a breeding ground for disorderly elements. Take, for instance, the possible fat man in that doorway; and, again, the possible bald man in that doorway. Are they the same possible man, or two possible men? How do we decide? How many possible men are there in that doorway? Are there more possible thin ones than fat ones? How many of them are alike? Or would their being alike make them one? Are no *two* possible things alike? Is this the same as saying that it is impossible for two things to be alike? Or, finally, is the concept of identity simply inapplicable to unactualized possibles? But what sense can be found in talking of entities which cannot meaningfully be said to be identical with themselves and distinct from one another? These elements are well-nigh incorrigible. By a Fregean therapy of individual concepts,[2] some effort might be made at rehabilitation; but I feel we'd do better simply to clear Wyman's slum and be done with it.

Possibility, along with the other modalities of necessity and impossibility and contingency, raises problems upon which I do not mean to imply that we should turn our backs. But we can at least limit modalities to whole statements. We may impose the adverb 'possibly' upon a statement as a whole, and we may well worry about the semantical analysis of such usage; but little real advance in such analysis is to be hoped for in expanding our universe to include so-called *possible entities*. I suspect that the main motive for this expansion is simply the old notion that Pegasus, for example, must be because otherwise it would be nonsense to say even that he is not.

Still, all the rank luxuriance of Wyman's universe of possibles would seem to come to naught when we make a slight change in the example and speak not of Pegasus but of the round square cupola on Berkeley College. If, unless Pegasus were, it would be nonsense to say that he is not, then by the same token, unless the round square cupola on Berkeley College were, it

---

[2] See below, p. 152.

would be nonsense to say that it is not. But, unlike Pegasus, the round square cupola on Berkeley College cannot be admitted even as an unactualized *possible*. Can we drive Wyman now to admitting also a realm of unactualizable impossibles? If so, a good many embarrassing questions could be asked about them. We might hope even to trap Wyman in contradictions, by getting him to admit that certain of these entities are at once round and square. But the wily Wyman chooses the other horn of the dilemma and concedes that it is nonsense to say that the round square cupola on Berkeley College is not. He says that the phrase 'round square cupola' is meaningless.

Wyman was not the first to embrace this alternative. The doctrine of the meaninglessness of contradictions runs away back. The tradition survives, moreover, in writers who seem to share none of Wyman's motivations. Still, I wonder whether the first temptation to such a doctrine may not have been substantially the motivation which we have observed in Wyman. Certainly the doctrine has no intrinsic appeal; and it has led its devotees to such quixotic extremes as that of challenging the method of proof by *reductio ad absurdum*—a challenge in which I sense a *reductio ad absurdum* of the doctrine itself.

Moreover, the doctrine of meaninglessness of contradictions has the severe methodological drawback that it makes it impossible, in principle, ever to devise an effective test of what is meaningful and what is not. It would be forever impossible for us to devise systematic ways of deciding whether a string of signs made sense—even to us individually, let alone other people—or not. For it follows from a discovery in mathematical logic, due to Church [2], that there can be no generally applicable test of contradictoriness.

I have spoken disparagingly of Plato's beard, and hinted that it is tangled. I have dwelt at length on the inconveniences of putting up with it. It is time to think about taking steps.

Russell, in his theory of so-called singular descriptions, showed clearly how we might meaningfully use seeming names without supposing that there be the entities allegedly named. The names to which Russell's theory directly applies are complex descriptive names such as 'the author of *Waverley*', 'the present King of France', 'the round square cupola on Berkeley College'. Russell analyzes such phrases systematically as fragments of the whole sentences in which they occur. The sentence 'The author of *Waverley* was a poet', for example, is explained as a whole as meaning 'Someone (better: something) wrote *Waverley* and was a poet, and nothing else wrote *Waverley*'. (The point of this added clause is to affirm the uniqueness which is implicit in the word 'the', in '*the* author of *Waverley*'.) The sentence 'The round square cupola on Berkeley College is pink' is explained as 'Something is round and square and is a cupola on Berkeley College and is pink, and nothing else is round and square and a cupola on Berkeley College'.[3]

The virtue of this analysis is that the seeming name, a descriptive phrase, is paraphrased *in context* as a so-called incomplete symbol. No unified expression is offered as an analysis of the descriptive phrase, but the statement as a whole which was the context of that phrase still gets its full quota of meaning—whether true or false.

The unanalyzed statement 'The author of *Waverley* was a poet' contains a part, 'the author of *Waverley*', which is wrongly supposed by McX and Wyman to demand objective reference in order to be meaningful at all. But in Russell's translation, 'Something wrote *Waverley* and was a poet and nothing else wrote *Waverley*', the burden of objective reference which had been put upon the descriptive phrase is now taken over by words of the kind that logicians call bound variables, variables of quantification, namely, words like 'something', 'nothing', 'everything'. These words, far from purporting to be names specifically of the author of *Waverley*, do not purport to be names at all; they refer to entities generally, with a kind of studied ambiguity peculiar to themselves.[4] These quantificational words or bound variables are, of course a basic part of language, and their meaningfulness, at least in context, is not

---

[3] For more on the theory of descriptions see below, pp. 85f, 166f.

[4] For more explicit treatment of the bound variable see below, pp. 82, 102f.

to be challenged. But their meaningfulness in no way presupposes there being either the author of *Waverley* or the round square cupola on Berkeley College or any other specifically preassigned objects.

Where descriptions are concerned, there is no longer any difficulty in affirming or denying being. 'There *is* the author of *Waverley*' is explained by Russell as meaning 'Someone (or, more strictly, something) wrote *Waverley* and nothing else wrote *Waverley*'. 'The author of *Waverley* is not' is explained, correspondingly, as the alternation 'Either each thing failed to write *Waverley* or two or more things wrote *Waverley*'. This alternation is false, but meaningful; and it contains no expression purporting to name the author of *Waverley*. The statement 'The round square cupola on Berkeley College is not' is analyzed in similar fashion. So the old notion that statements of nonbeing defeat themselves goes by the board. When a statement of being or nonbeing is analyzed by Russell's theory of descriptions, it ceases to contain any expression which even purports to name the alleged entity whose being is in question, so that the meaningfulness of the statement no longer can be thought to presuppose that there be such an entity.

Now what of 'Pegasus'? This being a word rather than a descriptive phrase, Russell's argument does not immediately apply to it. However, it can easily be made to apply. We have only to rephrase 'Pegasus' as a description, in any way that seems adequately to single out our idea; say, 'the winged horse that was captured by Bellerophon'. Substituting such a phrase for 'Pegasus', we can then proceed to analyze the statement 'Pegasus is', or 'Pegasus is not', precisely on the analogy of Russell's analysis of 'The author of *Waverley* is' and 'The author of *Waverley* is not'.

In order thus to subsume a one-word name or alleged name such as 'Pegasus' under Russell's theory of description, we must, of course, be able first to translate the word into a description. But this is no real restriction. If the notion of Pegasus had been so obscure or so basic a one that no pat translation into a descriptive phrase had offered itself along familiar lines, we could still have availed ourselves of the following artificial and trivial-seeming device: we could have appealed to the *ex hypothesi* unanalyzable, irreducible attribute of *being Pegasus*, adopting, for its expression, the verb 'is-Pegasus', or 'pegasizes'. The noun 'Pegasus' itself could then be treated as derivative, and identified after all with a description: 'the thing that is-Pegasus', 'the thing that pegasizes'.[5]

If the importing of such a predicate as 'pegasizes' seems to commit us to recognizing that there is a corresponding attribute, pegasizing, in Plato's heaven or in the minds of men, well and good. Neither we nor Wyman nor McX have been contending, thus far, about the being or nonbeing of universals, but rather about that of Pegasus. If in terms of pegasizing we can interpret the noun 'Pegasus' as a description subject to Russell's theory of descriptions, then we have disposed of the old notion that Pegasus cannot be said not to be without presupposing that in some sense Pegasus is.

Our argument is now quite general. McX and Wyman supposed that we could not meaningfully affirm a statement of the form 'So-and-so is not', with a simple or descriptive singular noun in place of 'so-and-so', unless so-and-so is. This supposition is now seen to be quite generally groundless, since the singular noun in question can always be expanded into a singular description, trivially or otherwise, and then analyzed out *à la* Russell.

We commit ourselves to an ontology containing numbers when we say there are prime numbers larger than a million; we commit ourselves to an ontology containing centaurs when we say there are centaurs; and we commit ourselves to an ontology containing Pegasus when we say Pegasus is. But we do not commit ourselves to an ontology containing Pegasus or the author of *Waverley* or the round square cupola on Berkeley College when we say that Pegasus or the author of *Waverley* or the cupola in question is *not*. We need no longer labor under the delusion that the meaningfulness of a statement containing

---

[5] For further remarks on such assimilation of all singular terms to descriptions see below, p. 167; also Quine [2], pp. 218–224.

a singular term presupposes an entity named by the term. A singular term need not name to be significant.

An inkling of this might have dawned on Wyman and McX even without benefit of Russell if they had only noticed—as so few of us do—that there is a gulf between *meaning* and *naming* even in the case of a singular term which is genuinely a name of an object. The following example from Frege [3] will serve. The phrase 'Evening Star' names a certain large physical object of spherical form, which is hurtling through space some scores of millions of miles from here. The phrase 'Morning Star' names the same thing, as was probably first established by some observant Babylonian. But the two phrases cannot be regarded as having the same meaning; otherwise that Babylonian could have dispensed with his observations and contented himself with reflecting on the meanings of his words. The meanings, then, being different from one another, must be other than the named object, which is one and the same in both cases.

Confusion of meaning with naming not only made McX think he could not meaningfully repudiate Pegasus; a continuing confusion of meaning with naming no doubt helped engender his absurd notion that Pegasus is an idea, a mental entity. The structure of his confusion is as follows. He confused the alleged *named object* Pegasus with the *meaning* of the word 'Pegasus', therefore concluding that Pegasus must be in order that the word have meaning. But what sorts of things are meanings? This is a moot point; however, one might quite plausibly explain meanings as ideas in the mind, supposing we can make clear sense in turn of the idea of ideas in the mind. Therefore Pegasus, initially confused with a meaning, ends up as an idea in the mind. It is the more remarkable that Wyman, subject to the same initial motivation as McX, should have avoided this particular blunder and wound up with unactualized possibles instead.

Now let us turn to the ontological problem of universals: the question whether there are such entities as attributes, relations, classes, numbers, functions. McX, characteristically enough, thinks there are. Speaking of attributes, he says: "There

are red houses, red roses, red sunsets; this much is prephilo-
sophical common sense in which we must all agree. These houses,
roses, and sunsets, then, have something in common; and this
which they have in common is all I mean by the attribute of
redness." For McX, thus, there being attributes is even more
obvious and trivial than the obvious and trivial fact of there
being red houses, roses, and sunsets. This, I think, is characteristic of metaphysics, or at least of that part of metaphysics
called ontology: one who regards a statement on this subject
as true at all must regard it as trivially true. One's ontology is
basic to the conceptual scheme by which he interprets all
experiences, even the most commonplace ones. Judged within
some particular conceptual scheme—and how else is judgment
possible?—an ontological statement goes without saying, standing in need of no separate justification at all. Ontological statements follow immediately from all manner of casual statements
of commonplace fact, just as—from the point of view, anyway,
of McX's conceptual scheme—'There is an attribute' follows
from 'There are red houses, red roses, red sunsets'.

Judged in another conceptual scheme, an ontological statement which is axiomatic to McX's mind may, with equal im-
mediacy and triviality, be adjudged false. One may admit that
there are red houses, roses, and sunsets, but deny, except as a
popular and misleading manner of speaking, that they have
anything in common. The words 'houses', 'roses', and 'sunsets'
are true of sundry individual entities which are houses and
roses and sunsets, and the word 'red' or 'red object' is true of
each of sundry individual entities which are red houses, red
roses, red sunsets; but there is not, in addition, any entity
whatever, individual or otherwise, which is named by the word
'redness', nor, for that matter, by the word 'householood', 'rose-
hood', 'sunsethood'. That the houses and roses and sunsets are
all of them red may be taken as ultimate and irreducible, and
it may be held that McX is no better off, in point of real explanatory power, for all the occult entities which he posits under such names as 'redness'.

One means by which McX might naturally have tried to

impose his ontology of universals on us was already removed before we turned to the problem of universals. McX cannot argue that predicates such as 'red' or 'is-red', which we all concur in using, must be regarded as names each of a single universal entity in order that they be meaningful at all. For we have seen that being a name of something is a much more special feature than being meaningful. He cannot even charge us—at least not by *that* argument—with having posited an attribute of pegasizing by our adoption of the predicate 'pegasizes'.

However, McX hits upon a different strategem. "Let us grant," he says, "this distinction between meaning and naming of which you make so much. Let us even grant that 'is red', 'pegasizes', etc., are not names of attributes. Still, you admit they have meanings. But these *meanings*, whether they are *named* or not, are still universals, and I venture to say that some of them might even be the very things that I call attributes, or something to much the same purpose in the end."

For McX, this is an unusually penetrating speech; and the only way I know to counter it is by refusing to admit meanings. However, I feel no reluctance toward refusing to admit meanings, for I do not thereby deny that words and statements are meaningful. McX and I may agree to the letter in our classification of linguistic forms into the meaningful and the meaningless, even though McX construes meaningfulness as the *having* (in some sense of 'having') of some abstract entity which he calls a meaning, whereas I do not. I remain free to maintain that the fact that a given linguistic utterance is meaningful (or *significant*, as I prefer to say so as not to invite hypostasis of meanings as entities) is an ultimate and irreducible matter of fact; or, I may undertake to analyze it in terms directly of what people do in the presence of the linguistic utterance in question and other utterances similar to it.

The useful ways in which people ordinarily talk or seem to talk about meanings boil down to two: the *having* of meanings, which is significance, and *sameness* of meaning, or synonomy. What is called *giving* the meaning of an utterance is simply the uttering of a synonym, couched, ordinarily, in clearer language than the original. If we are allergic to meanings as such, we can speak directly of utterances as significant or insignificant, and as synonymous or heteronymous one with another. The problem of explaining these adjectives 'significant' and 'synonymous' with some degree of clarity and rigor—preferably, as I see it, in terms of behavior—is as difficult as it is important.[6] But the explanatory value of special and irreducible intermediary entities called meanings is surely illusory.

Up to now I have argued that we can use singular terms significantly in sentences without presupposing that there are the entities which those terms purport to name. I have argued further that we can use general terms, for example, predicates, without conceding them to be names of abstract entities. I have argued further that we can view utterances as significant, and as synonymous or heteronymous with one another, without countenancing a realm of entities called meanings. At this point McX begins to wonder whether there is any limit at all to our ontological immunity. Does *nothing* we may say commit us to the assumption of universals or other entities which we may find unwelcome?

I have already suggested a negative answer to this question, in speaking of bound variables, or variables of quantification, in connection with Russell's theory of descriptions. We can very easily involve ourselves in ontological commitments by saying, for example, that *there is something* (bound variable) which red houses and sunsets have in common; or that *there is something* which is a prime number larger than a million. But this is, essentially, the *only* way we can involve ourselves in ontological commitments: by our use of bound variables. The use of alleged names is no criterion, for we can repudiate their namehood at the drop of a hat unless the assumption of a corresponding entity can be spotted in the things we affirm in terms of bound variables. Names are, in fact, altogether immaterial to the ontological issue, for I have shown, in connection with 'Pegasus' and 'pegasize', that names can be converted to descriptions, and Russell has shown that descriptions can be eliminated.

[6] See Essays II and III.

Whatever we say with the help of names can be said in a language which shuns names altogether. To be assumed as an entity is, purely and simply, to be reckoned as the value of a variable. In terms of the categories of traditional grammar, this amounts roughly to saying that to be is to be in the range of reference of a pronoun. Pronouns are the basic media of reference; nouns might better have been named propronouns. The variables of quantification, 'something', 'nothing', 'everything', range over our whole ontology, whatever it may be; and we are convicted of a particular ontological presupposition if, and only if, the alleged presuppositum has to be reckoned among the entities over which our variables range in order to render one of our affirmations true.

We may say, for example, that some dogs are white and not thereby commit ourselves to recognizing either doghood or whiteness as entities. 'Some dogs are white' says that some things that are dogs are white; and, in order that this statement be true, the things over which the bound variable 'something' ranges must include some white dogs, but need not include doghood or whiteness. On the other hand, when we say that some zoölogical species are cross-fertile we are committing ourselves to recognizing as entities the several species themselves, abstract though they are. We remain so committed at least until we devise some way of so paraphrasing the statement as to show that the seeming reference to species on the part of our bound variable was an avoidable manner of speaking.[7]

Classical mathematics, as the example of primes larger than a million clearly illustrates, is up to its neck in commitments to an ontology of abstract entities. Thus it is that the great mediaeval controversy over universals has flared up anew in the modern philosophy of mathematics. The issue is clearer now than of old, because we now have a more explicit standard whereby to decide what ontology a given theory or form of discourse is committed to: a theory is committed to those and only those entities to which the bound variables of the theory

[7] For more on this topic see Essay VI.

must be capable of referring in order that the affirmations made in the theory be true.

Because this standard of ontological presupposition did not emerge clearly in the philosophical tradition, the modern philosophical mathematicians have not on the whole recognized that they were debating the same old problem of universals in a newly clarified form. But the fundamental cleavages among modern points of view on foundations of mathematics do come down pretty explicitly to disagreements as to the range of entities to which the bound variables should be permitted to refer.

The three main mediaeval points of view regarding universals are designated by historians as *realism, conceptualism*, and *nominalism*. Essentially these same three doctrines reappear in twentieth-century surveys of the philosophy of mathematics under the new names *logicism, intuitionism*, and *formalism*.

Realism, as the word is used in connection with the mediaeval controversy over universals, is the Platonic doctrine that universals or abstract entities have being independently of the mind; the mind may discover them but cannot create them. *Logicism*, represented by Frege, Russell, Whitehead, Church, and Carnap, condones the use of bound variables to refer to abstract entities known and unknown, specifiable and unspecifiable, indiscriminately.

Conceptualism holds that there are universals but they are mind-made. *Intuitionism*, espoused in modern times in one form or another by Poincaré, Brouwer, Weyl, and others, countenances the use of bound variables to refer to abstract entities only when those entities are capable of being cooked up individually from ingredients specified in advance. As Fraenkel has put it, logicism holds that classes are discovered while intuitionism holds that they are invented—a fair statement indeed of the old opposition between realism and conceptualism. This opposition is no mere quibble; it makes an essential difference in the amount of classical mathematics to which one is willing to subscribe. Logicists, or realists, are able on their assumptions to get Cantor's ascending orders of infinity; intuitionists are compelled to stop with the lowest order of infinity, and, as an indirect consequence, to abandon even some of the classical laws of real numbers.[8] The modern controversy between logicism and intuitionism arose, in fact, from disagreements over infinity.

Formalism, associated with the name of Hilbert, echoes intuitionism in deploring the logicist's unbridled recourse to universals. But formalism also finds intuitionism unsatisfactory. This could happen for either of two opposite reasons. The formalist might, like the logicist, object to the crippling of classical mathematics; or he might, like the *nominalists* of old, object to admitting abstract entities at all, even in the restrained sense of mind-made entities. The upshot is the same: the formalist keeps classical mathematics as a play of insignificant notations. This play of notations can still be of utility—whatever utility it has already shown itself to have as a crutch for physicists and technologists. But utility need not imply significance, in any literal linguistic sense. Nor need the marked success of mathematicians in spinning out theorems, and in finding objective bases for agreement with one another's results, imply significance. For an adequate basis for agreement among mathematicians can be found simply in the rules which govern the manipulation of the notations—these syntactical rules being, unlike the notations themselves, quite significant and intelligible.[9]

I have argued that the sort of ontology we adopt can be consequential—notably in connection with mathematics, although this is only an example. Now how are we to adjudicate among rival ontologies? Certainly the answer is not provided by the semantical formula "To be is to be the value of a variable"; this formula serves rather, conversely, in testing the conformity of a given remark or doctrine to a prior ontological standard. We look to bound variables in connection with ontology not in order to know what there is, but in order to know what a given remark or doctrine, ours or someone else's, *says* there is;

[8] See below, pp. 125ff.
[9] See Goodman and Quine. For further discussion of the general matters touched on in the past two pages, see Bernays [1], Fraenkel, Black.

and this much is quite properly a problem involving language. But what there is is another question.

In debating over what there is, there are still reasons for operating on a semantical plane. One reason is to escape from the predicament noted at the beginning of this essay: the predicament of my not being able to admit that there are things which McX countenances and I do not. So long as I adhere to my ontology, as opposed to McX's, I cannot allow my bound variables to refer to entities which belong to McX's ontology and not to mine. I can, however, consistently describe our disagreement by characterizing the statements which McX affirms. Provided merely that my ontology countenances linguistic forms, or at least concrete inscriptions and utterances, I can talk about McX's sentences.

Another reason for withdrawing to a semantical plane is to find common ground on which to argue. Disagreement in ontology involves basic disagreement in conceptual schemes; yet McX and I, despite these basic disagreements, find that our conceptual schemes converge sufficiently in their intermediate and upper ramifications to enable us to communicate successfully on such topics as politics, weather, and, in particular, language. In so far as our basic controversy over ontology can be translated upward into a semantical controversy about words and what to do with them, the collapse of the controversy into question-begging may be delayed.

It is no wonder, then, that ontological controversy should tend into controversy over language. But we must not jump to the conclusion that what there is depends on words. Translatability of a question into semantical terms is no indication that the question is linguistic. To see Naples is to bear a name which, when prefixed to the words 'sees Naples', yields a true sentence; still there is nothing linguistic about seeing Naples.

Our acceptance of an ontology is, I think, similar in principle to our acceptance of a scientific theory, say a system of physics: we adopt, at least insofar as we are reasonable, the simplest conceptual scheme into which the disordered fragments of raw experience can be fitted and arranged. Our ontology is determined once we have fixed upon the over-all conceptual scheme which is to accommodate science in the broadest sense; and the considerations which determine a reasonable construction of any part of that conceptual scheme, for example, the biological or the physical part, are not different in kind from the considerations which determine a reasonable construction of the whole. To whatever extent the adoption of any system of scientific theory may be said to be a matter of language, the same—but no more—may be said of the adoption of an ontology.

But simplicity, as a guiding principle in constructing conceptual schemes, is not a clear and unambiguous idea; and it is quite capable of presenting a double or multiple standard. Imagine, for example, that we have devised the most economical set of concepts adequate to the play-by-play reporting of immediate experience. The entities under this scheme—the values of bound variables—are, let us suppose, individual subjective events of sensation or reflection. We should still find, no doubt, that a physicalistic conceptual scheme, purporting to talk about external objects, offers great advantages in simplifying our over-all reports. By bringing together scattered sense events and treating them as perceptions of one object, we reduce the complexity of our stream of experience to a manageable conceptual simplicity. The rule of simplicity is indeed our guiding maxim in assigning sense data to objects: we associate an earlier and a later round sensum with the same so-called penny, or with two different so-called pennies, in obedience to the demands of maximum simplicity in our total world-picture.

Here we have two competing conceptual schemes, a phenomenalistic one and a physicalistic one. Which should prevail? Each has its advantages; each has its special simplicity in its own way. Each, I suggest, deserves to be developed. Each may be said, indeed, to be the more fundamental, though in different senses: the one is epistemologically, the other physically, fundamental.

The physical conceptual scheme simplifies our account of experience because of the way myriad scattered sense events come to be associated with single so-called objects; still there is no likelihood that each sentence about physical objects can actually be translated, however deviously and complexly, into the phenomenalistic language. Physical objects are postulated entities which round out and simplify our account of the flux of experience, just as the introduction of irrational numbers simplifies laws of arithmetic. From the point of view of the conceptual scheme of the elementary arithmetic of rational numbers alone, the broader arithmetic of rational and irrational numbers would have the status of a convenient myth, simpler than the literal truth (namely, the arithmetic of rationals) and yet containing that literal truth as a scattered part. Similarly, from a phenomenalistic point of view, the conceptual scheme of physical objects is a convenient myth, simpler than the literal truth and yet containing that literal truth as a scattered part.[10]

Now what of classes or attributes of physical objects, in turn? A platonistic ontology of this sort is, from the point of view of a strictly physicalistic conceptual scheme, as much a myth as that physicalistic conceptual scheme itself is for phenomenalism. This higher myth is a good and useful one, in turn, in so far as it simplifies our account of physics. Since mathematics is an integral part of this higher myth, the utility of this myth for physical science is evident enough. In speaking of it nevertheless as a myth, I echo that philosophy of mathematics to which I alluded earlier under the name of formalism. But an attitude of formalism may with equal justice be adopted toward the physical conceptual scheme, in turn, by the pure aesthete or phenomenalist.

The analogy between the myth of mathematics and the myth of physics is, in some additional and perhaps fortuitous ways, strikingly close. Consider, for example, the crisis which was precipitated in the foundations of mathematics, at the turn of the century, by the discovery of Russell's paradox and other antinomies of set theory. These contradictions had to be obviated by unintuitive, *ad hoc* devices;[11] our mathematical myth-making became deliberate and evident to all. But what

---

[10] The arithmetical analogy is due to Frank, pp. 108f.
[11] See below, pp. 90ff, 96ff, 122ff.

of physics? An antinomy arose between the undular and the corpuscular accounts of light; and if this was not as out-and-out a contradiction as Russell's paradox, I suspect that the reason is that physics is not as out-and-out as mathematics. Again, the second great modern crisis in the foundations of mathematics—precipitated in 1931 by Gödel's proof [2] that there are bound to be undecidable statements in arithmetic—has its companion piece in physics in Heisenberg's indeterminacy principle.

In earlier pages I undertook to show that some common arguments in favor of certain ontologies are fallacious. Further, I advanced an explicit standard whereby to decide what the ontological commitments of a theory are. But the question what ontology actually to adopt still stands open, and the obvious counsel is tolerance and an experimental spirit. Let us by all means see how much of the physicalistic conceptual scheme can be reduced to a phenomenalistic one; still, physics also naturally demands pursuing, irreducible *in toto* though it be. Let us see how, or to what degree, natural science may be rendered independent of platonistic mathematics; but let us also pursue mathematics and delve into its platonistic foundations.

From among the various conceptual schemes best suited to these various pursuits, one—the phenomenalistic—claims epistemological priority. Viewed from within the phenomenalistic conceptual scheme, the ontologies of physical objects and mathematical objects are myths. The quality of myth, however, is relative; relative, in this case, to the epistemological point of view. This point of view is one among various, corresponding to one among our various interests and purposes.

II

TWO DOGMAS OF EMPIRICISM

Modern empiricism has been conditioned in large part by two dogmas. One is a belief in some fundamental cleavage between truths which are *analytic*, or grounded in meanings independently of matters of fact, and truths which are *synthetic*, or grounded in fact. The other dogma is *reductionism:* the belief that each meaningful statement is equivalent to some logical construct upon terms which refer to immediate experience. Both dogmas, I shall argue, are ill-founded. One effect of abandoning them is, as we shall see, a blurring of the supposed boundary between speculative metaphysics and natural science. Another effect is a shift toward pragmatism.

1. Background for Analyticity

Kant's cleavage between analytic and synthetic truths was foreshadowed in Hume's distinction between relations of ideas and matters of fact, and in Leibniz's distinction between truths of reason and truths of fact. Leibniz spoke of the truths of reason as true in all possible worlds. Picturesqueness aside, this is to say that the truths of reason are those which could not possibly be false. In the same vein we hear analytic statements defined as statements whose denials are self-contradictory. But this definition has small explanatory value; for the notion of self-contradictoriness, in the quite broad sense needed for this definition of analyticity, stands in exactly the same need of clarification as does the notion of analyticity itself. The two notions are the two sides of a single dubious coin.

Kant conceived of an analytic statement as one that attributes to its subject no more than is already conceptually contained

20

in the subject. This formulation has two shortcomings: it limits itself to statements of subject-predicate form, and it appeals to a notion of containment which is left at a metaphorical level. But Kant's intent, evident more from the use he makes of the notion of analyticity than from his definition of it, can be restated thus: a statement is analytic when it is true by virtue of meanings and independently of fact. Pursuing this line, let us examine the concept of *meaning* which is presupposed.

Meaning, let us remember, is not to be identified with naming.[1] Frege's example of 'Evening Star' and 'Morning Star', and Russell's of 'Scott' and 'the author of *Waverley*', illustrate that terms can name the same thing but differ in meaning. The distinction between meaning and naming is no less important at the level of abstract terms. The terms '9' and 'the number of the planets' name one and the same abstract entity but presumably must be regarded as unlike in meaning; for astronomical observation was needed, and not mere reflection on meanings, to determine the sameness of the entity in question.

The above examples consist of singular terms, concrete and abstract. With general terms, or predicates, the situation is somewhat different but parallel. Whereas a singular term purports to name an entity, abstract or concrete, a general term does not; but a general term is *true of* an entity, or of each of many, or of none.[2] The class of all entities of which a general term is true is called the *extension* of the term. Now paralleling the contrast between the meaning of a singular term and the entity named, we must distinguish equally between the meaning of a general term and its extension. The general terms 'creature with a heart' and 'creature with kidneys', for example, are perhaps alike in extension but unlike in meaning.

Confusion of meaning with extension, in the case of general terms, is less common than confusion of meaning with naming in the case of singular terms. It is indeed a commonplace in philosophy to oppose intension (or meaning) to extension, or, in a variant vocabulary, connotation to denotation.

[1] See above, p. 9.
[2] See above, p. 10, and below, pp. 107–115.

The Aristotelian notion of essence was the forerunner, no doubt, of the modern notion of intension or meaning. For Aristotle it was essential in men to be rational, accidental to be two-legged. But there is an important difference between this attitude and the doctrine of meaning. From the latter point of view it may indeed be conceded (if only for the sake of argument) that rationality is involved in the meaning of the word 'man' while two-leggedness is not; but two-leggedness may at the same time be viewed as involved in the meaning of 'biped' while rationality is not. Thus from the point of view of the doctrine of meaning it makes no sense to say of the actual individual, who is at once a man and a biped, that his rationality is essential and his two-leggedness accidental or vice versa. Things had essences, for Aristotle, but only linguistic forms have meanings. Meaning is what essence becomes when it is divorced from the object of reference and wedded to the word.

For the theory of meaning a conspicuous question is the nature of its objects: what sort of things are meanings? A felt need for meant entities may derive from an earlier failure to appreciate that meaning and reference are distinct. Once the theory of meaning is sharply separated from the theory of reference, it is a short step to recognizing as the primary business of the theory of meaning simply the synonymy of linguistic forms and the analyticity of statements; meanings themselves, as obscure intermediary entities, may well be abandoned.[3]

The problem of analyticity then confronts us anew. Statements which are analytic by general philosophical acclaim are not, indeed, far to seek. They fall into two classes. Those of the first class, which may be called *logically true*, are typified by:

(1)   No unmarried man is married.

The relevant feature of this example is that it not merely is true as it stands, but remains true under any and all reinterpretations of 'man' and 'married'. If we suppose a prior inventory of *logical* particles, comprising 'no', 'un-', 'not', 'if', 'then', 'and', etc., then in general a logical truth is a statement which is true

---

[3] See above, pp. 11f, and below, pp. 48f.

and remains true under all reinterpretations of its components
other than the logical particles.

But there is also a second class of analytic statements,
typified by:

(2)　　　　　　　　No bachelor is married.

The characteristic of such a statement is that it can be turned
into a logical truth by putting synonyms for synonyms; thus
(2) can be turned into (1) by putting 'unmarried man' for its
synonym 'bachelor'. We still lack a proper characterization of
this second class of analytic statements, and therewith of analyticity generally, inasmuch as we have had in the above description to lean on a notion of "synonymy" which is no less in need
of clarification than analyticity itself.

In recent years Carnap has tended to explain analyticity
by appeal to what he calls state-descriptions.[4] A state-description is any exhaustive assignment of truth values to the atomic,
or noncompound, statements of the language. All other statements of the language are, Carnap assumes, built up of their
component clauses by means of the familiar logical devices, in
such a way that the truth value of any complex statement is
fixed for each state-description by specifiable logical laws. A
statement is then explained as analytic when it comes out true
under every state description. This account is an adaptation of
Leibniz's "true in all possible worlds." But note that this version
of analyticity serves its purpose only if the atomic statements of
the language are, unlike 'John is a bachelor' and 'John is married', mutually independent. Otherwise there would be a state-
description which assigned truth to 'John is a bachelor' and to
'John is married', and consequently 'No bachelors are married'
would turn out synthetic rather than analytic under the proposed criterion. Thus the criterion of analyticity in terms of
state-descriptions serves only for languages devoid of extralogical synonym-pairs, such as 'bachelor' and 'unmarried man'—
synonym-pairs of the type which give rise to the "second class"
of analytic statements. The criterion in terms of state-descrip-

[4] Carnap [3], pp. 9ff; [4], pp. 70ff.

tions is a reconstruction at best of logical truth, not of analyticity.

I do not mean to suggest that Carnap is under any illusions on this point. His simplified model language with its state-descriptions is aimed primarily not at the general problem of analyticity but at another purpose, the clarification of probability and induction. Our problem, however, is analyticity; and here the major difficulty lies not in the first class of analytic statements, the logical truths, but rather in the second class, which depends on the notion of synonymy.

2. Definition

There are those who find it soothing to say that the analytic statements of the second class reduce to those of the first class, the logical truths, by *definition*; 'bachelor', for example, is *defined* as 'unmarried man'. But how de we find that 'bachelor' is defined as 'unmarried man'? Who defined it thus, and when? Are we to appeal to the nearest dictionary, and accept the lexicographer's formulation as law? Clearly this would be to put the cart before the horse. The lexicographer is an empirical scientist, whose business is the recording of antecedent facts; and if he glosses 'bachelor' as 'unmarried man' it is because of his belief that there is a relation of synonymy between those forms, implicit in general or preferred usage prior to his own work. The notion of synonymy presupposed here has still to be clarified, presumably in terms relating to linguistic behavior. Certainly the "definition" which is the lexicographer's report of an observed synonymy cannot be taken as the ground of the synonymy.

Definition is not, indeed, an activity exclusively of philologists. Philosophers and scientists frequently have occasion to "define" a recondite term by paraphrasing it into terms of a more familiar vocabulary. But ordinarily such a definition, like the philologist's, is pure lexicography, affirming a relation of synonymy antecedent to the exposition in hand.

Just what it means to affirm synonymy, just what the interconnections may be which are necessary and sufficient in order that two linguistic forms be properly describable as synonymous, is far from clear; but, whatever these interconnections may be, ordinarily they are grounded in usage. Definitions reporting selected instances of synonymy come then as reports upon usage.

There is also, however, a variant type of definitional activity which does not limit itself to the reporting of preëxisting synonymies. I have in mind what Carnap calls *explication*—an activity to which philosophers are given, and scientists also in their more philosophical moments. In explication the purpose is not merely to paraphrase the definiendum into an outright synonym, but actually to improve upon the definiendum by refining or supplementing its meaning. But even explication, though not merely reporting a preëxisting synonymy between definiendum and definiens, does rest nevertheless on *other* preexisting synonymies. The matter may be viewed as follows. Any word worth explicating has some contexts which, as wholes, are clear and precise enough to be useful; and the purpose of explication is to preserve the usage of these favored contexts while sharpening the usage of other contexts. In order that a given definition be suitable for purposes of explication, therefore, what is required is not that the definiendum in its antecedent usage be synonymous with the definiens, but just that each of these favored contexts of the definiendum, taken as a whole in its antecedent usage, be synonymous with the corresponding context of the definiens.

Two alternative definientia may be equally appropriate for the purposes of a given task of explication and yet not be synonymous with each other; for they may serve interchangeably within the favored contexts but diverge elsewhere. By cleaving to one of these definientia rather than the other, a definition of explicative kind generates, by fiat, a relation of synonymy between definiendum and definiens which did not hold before. But such a definition still owes its explicative function, as seen, to preexisting synonymies.

There does, however, remain still an extreme sort of definition which does not hark back to prior synonymies at all: namely, the explicitly conventional introduction of novel notations for purposes of sheer abbreviation. Here the definiendum becomes synonymous with the definiens simply because it has been created expressly for the purpose of being synonymous with the definiens. Here we have a really transparent case of synonymy created by definition; would that all species of synonymy were as intelligible. For the rest, definition rests on synonymy rather than explaining it.

The word 'definition' has come to have a dangerously reassuring sound, owing no doubt to its frequent occurrence in logical and mathematical writings. We shall do well to digress now into a brief appraisal of the role of definition in formal work.

In logical and mathematical systems either of two mutually antagonistic types of economy may be striven for, and each has its peculiar practical utility. On the one hand we may seek economy of practical expression—ease and brevity in the statement of multifarious relations. This sort of economy calls usually for distinctive concise notations for a wealth of concepts. Second, however, and oppositely, we may seek economy in grammar and vocabulary; we may try to find a minimum of basic concepts such that, once a distinctive notation has been appropriated to each of them, it becomes possible to express any desired further concept by mere combination and iteration of our basic notations. This second sort of economy is impractical in one way, since a poverty in basic idioms tends to a necessary lengthening of discourse. But it is practical in another way: it greatly simplifies theoretical discourse *about* the language, through minimizing the terms and the forms of construction wherein the language consists.

Both sorts of economy, though prima facie incompatible, are valuable in their separate ways. The custom has consequently arisen of combining both sorts of economy by forging in effect two languages, the one a part of the other. The inclusive language, though redundant in grammar and vocabulary, is economical in message lengths, while the part, called primitive notation, is economical in grammar and vocabulary. Whole and part are correlated by rules of translation whereby each idiom not in primitive notation is equated to some complex built up of primitive notation. These rules of translation are the so-called *definitions* which appear in formalized systems. They are best viewed not as adjuncts to one language but as correlations between two languages, the one a part of the other.

But these correlations are not arbitrary. They are supposed to show how the primitive notations can accomplish all purposes, save brevity and convenience, of the redundant language. Hence the definiendum and its definiens may be expected, in each case, to be related in one or another of the three ways lately noted. The definiens may be a faithful paraphrase of the definiendum into the narrower notation, preserving a direct synonymy[5] as of antecedent usage; or the definiens may, in the spirit of explication, improve upon the antecedent usage of the definiendum; or finally, the definiendum may be a newly created notation, newly endowed with meaning here and now.

In formal and informal work alike, thus, we find that definition—except in the extreme case of the explicitly conventional introduction of new notations—hinges on prior relations of synonymy. Recognizing then that the notion of definition does not hold the key to synonymy and analyticity, let us look further into synonymy and say no more of definition.

3. Interchangeability

A natural suggestion, deserving close examination, is that the synonymy of two linguistic forms consists simply in their interchangeability in all contexts without change of truth value —interchangeability, in Leibniz's phrase, *salva veritate*.[6] Note that synonyms so conceived need not even be free from vagueness, as long as the vaguenesses match.

[5] According to an important variant sense of 'definition', the relation preserved may be the weaker relation of mere agreement in reference; see below, p. 132. But definition in this sense is better ignored in the present connection, being irrelevant to the question of synonymy.

[6] Cf. Lewis [1], p. 373.

But it is not quite true that the synonyms 'bachelor' and 'unmarried man' are everywhere interchangeable *salva veritate*. Truths which become false under substitution of 'unmarried man' for 'bachelor' are easily constructed with the help of 'bachelor of arts' or 'bachelor's buttons'; also with the help of quotation, thus:

'Bachelor' has less than ten letters.

Such counterinstances can, however, perhaps be set aside by treating the phrases 'bachelor of arts' and 'bachelor's buttons' and the quotation ' 'bachelor' ' each as a single indivisible word and then stipulating that the interchangeability *salva veritate* which is to be the touchstone of synonymy is not supposed to apply to fragmentary occurrences inside of a word. This account of synonymy, supposing it acceptable on other counts, has indeed the drawback of appealing to a prior conception of "word" which can be counted on to present difficulties of formulation in its turn. Nevertheless some progress might be claimed in having reduced the problem of synonymy to a problem of word-hood. Let us pursue this line a bit, taking "word" for granted.

The question remains whether interchangeability *salva veritate* (apart from occurrences within words) is a strong enough condition for synonymy, or whether, on the contrary, some heteronymous expressions might be thus interchangeable. Now let us be clear that we are not concerned here with synonymy in the sense of complete identity in psychological associations or poetic quality; indeed no two expressions are synonymous in such a sense. We are concerned only with what may be called *cognitive* synonymy. Just what this is cannot be said without successfully finishing the present study; but we know something about it from the need which arose for it in connection with analyticity in §1. The sort of synonymy needed there was merely such that any analytic statement could be turned into a logical truth by putting synonyms for synonyms. Turning the tables and assuming analyticity, indeed, we could explain cognitive synonymy of terms as follows (keeping to the familiar example): to say that 'bachelor' and 'unmarried man' are cognitively synonymous is to say no more nor less than that the statement:

(3)   All and only bachelors are unmarried men

is analytic.[7]

What we need is an account of cognitive synonymy not presupposing analyticity—if we are to explain analyticity conversely with help of cognitive synonymy as undertaken in §1. And indeed such an independent account of cognitive synonymy is at present up for consideration, namely, interchangeability *salva veritate* everywhere except within words. The question before us, to resume the thread at last, is whether such interchangeability is a sufficient condition for cognitive synonymy. We can quickly assure ourselves that it is, by examples of the following sort. The statement:

(4)   Necessarily all and only bachelors are bachelors

is evidently true, even supposing 'necessarily' so narrowly construed as to be truly applicable only to analytic statements. Then, if 'bachelor' and 'unmarried man' are interchangeable *salva veritate*, the result:

(5)   Necessarily all and only bachelors are unmarried men

of putting 'unmarried man' for an occurrence of 'bachelor' in (4) must, like (4), be true. But to say that (5) is true is to say that (3) is analytic, and hence that 'bachelor' and 'unmarried man' are cognitively synonymous.

Let us see what there is about the above argument that gives it its air of hocus-pocus. The condition of interchangeability *salva veritate* varies in its force with variations in the richness of the language at hand. The above argument supposes we are working with a language rich enough to contain the adverb 'necessarily', this adverb being so construed as to yield truth

[7] This is cognitive synonymy in a primary, broad sense. Carnap ([3], pp. 56ff) and Lewis ([2], pp. 83ff) have suggested how, once this notion is at hand, a narrower sense of cognitive synonymy which is preferable for some purposes can in turn be derived. But this special ramification of concept-building lies aside from the present purposes and must not be confused with the broad sort of cognitive synonymy here concerned.

when and only when applied to an analytic statement. But can we condone a language which contains such an adverb? Does the adverb really make sense? To suppose that it does is to suppose that we have already made satisfactory sense of 'analytic'. Then what are we so hard at work on right now?

Our argument is not flatly circular, but something like it. It has the form, figuratively speaking, of a closed curve in space.

Interchangeability *salva veritate* is meaningless until relativized to a language whose extent is specified in relevant respects. Suppose now we consider a language containing just the following materials. There is an indefinitely large stock of one-place predicates (for example, 'F' where 'Fx' means that x is a man) and many-place predicates (for example, 'G' where 'Gxy' means that x loves y), mostly having to do with extralogical subject matter. The rest of the language is logical. The atomic sentences consist each of a predicate followed by one or more variables 'x', 'y', etc.; and the complex sentences are built up of the atomic ones by truth functions ('not', 'and', 'or', etc.) and quantification.[8] In effect such a language enjoys the benefits also of descriptions and indeed singular terms generally, these being contextually definable in known ways.[9] Even abstract singular terms naming classes, classes of classes, etc., are contextually definable in case the assumed stock of predicates includes the two-place predicate of class membership.[10] Such a language can be adequate to classical mathematics and indeed to scientific discourse generally, except in so far as the latter involves debatable devices such as contrary-to-fact conditionals or modal adverbs like 'necessarily'.[11] Now a language of this type is extensional, in this sense: any two predicates which agree extensionally (that is, are true of the same objects) are interchangeable *salva veritate*.[12]

---

[8] Pp. 81ff, below, contain a description of just such a language, except that there happens there to be just one predicate, the two-place predicate 'ϵ'.

[9] See above, pp. 5–8; also below, pp. 85f, 166f.

[10] See below, p. 87.

[11] On such devices see also Essay VIII.

[12] This is the substance of Quine [1], *121.

In an extensional language, therefore, interchangeability *salva veritate* is no assurance of cognitive synonymy of the desired type. That 'bachelor' and 'unmarried man' are interchangeable *salva veritate* in an extensional language assures us of no more than that (3) is true. There is no assurance here that the extensional agreement of 'bachelor' and 'unmarried man' rests on meaning rather than merely on accidental matters of fact, as does the extensional agreement of 'creature with a heart' and 'creature with kidneys'.

For most purposes extensional agreement is the nearest approximation to synonymy we need care about. But the fact remains that extensional agreement falls far short of cognitive synonymy of the type required for explaining analyticity in the manner of §1. The type of cognitive synonymy required there is such as to equate the synonymy of 'bachelor' and 'unmarried man' with the analyticity of (3), not merely with the truth of (3).

So we must recognize that interchangeability *salva veritate*, if construed in relation to an extensional language, is not a sufficient condition of cognitive synonymy in the sense needed for deriving analyticity in the manner of §1. If a language contains an intensional adverb 'necessarily' in the sense lately noted, or other particles to the same effect, then interchangeability *salva veritate* in such a language does afford a sufficient condition of cognitive synonymy; but such a language is intelligible only in so far as the notion of analyticity is already understood in advance.

The effort to explain cognitive synonymy first, for the sake of deriving analyticity from it afterward as in §1, is perhaps the wrong approach. Instead we might try explaining analyticity somehow without appeal to cognitive synonymy. Afterward we could doubtless derive cognitive synonymy from analyticity satisfactorily enough if desired. We have seen that cognitive synonymy of 'bachelor' and 'unmarried man' can be explained as analyticity of (3). The same explanation works for any pair of one-place predicates, of course, and it can be extended in obvious fashion to many-place predicates. Other syntactical categories can also be accommodated in fairly parallel fashion.

Singular terms may be said to be cognitively synonymous when the statement of identity formed by putting '=' between them is analytic. Statements may be said simply to be cognitively synonymous when their biconditional (the result of joining them by 'if and only if') is analytic.[13] If we care to lump all categories into a single formulation, at the expense of assuming again the notion of "word" which was appealed to early in this section, we can describe any two linguistic forms as cognitively synonymous when the two forms are interchangeable (apart from occurrences within "words") *salva* (no longer *veritate* but) *analyticitate*. Certain technical questions arise, indeed, over cases of ambiguity or homonymy; let us not pause for them, however, for we are already digressing. Let us rather turn our backs on the problem of synonymy and address ourselves anew to that of analyticity.

4. Semantical Rules

Analyticity at first seemed most naturally definable by appeal to a realm of meanings. On refinement, the appeal to meanings gave way to an appeal to synonymy or definition. But definition turned out to be a will-o'-the-wisp, and synonymy turned out to be best understood only by dint of a prior appeal to analyticity itself. So we are back at the problem of analyticity.

I do not know whether the statement 'Everything green is extended' is analytic. Now does my indecision over this example really betray an incomplete understanding, an incomplete grasp of the "meanings", of 'green' and 'extended'? I think not. The trouble is not with 'green' or 'extended', but with 'analytic'.

It is often hinted that the difficulty in separating analytic statements from synthetic ones in ordinary language is due to the vagueness of ordinary language and that the distinction is clear when we have a precise artificial language with explicit "semantical rules." This, however, as I shall now attempt to show, is a confusion.

[13] The 'if and only if' itself is intended in the truth functional sense. See Carnap [3], p. 14.

The notion of analyticity about which we are worrying is a purported relation between statements and languages: a statement S is said to be *analytic for* a language L, and the problem is to make sense of this relation generally, that is, for variable 'S' and 'L'. The gravity of this problem is not perceptibly less for artificial languages than for natural ones. The problem of making sense of the idiom 'S is analytic for L', with variable 'S' and 'L', retains its stubbornness even if we limit the range of the variable 'L' to artificial languages. Let me now try to make this point evident.

For artificial languages and semantical rules we look naturally to the writings of Carnap. His semantical rules take various forms, and to make my point I shall have to distinguish certain of the forms. Let us suppose, to begin with, an artificial language L_0 whose semantical rules have the form explicitly of a specification, by recursion or otherwise, of all the analytic statements of L_0. The rules tell us that such and such statements, and only those, are the analytic statements of L_0. Now here the difficulty is simply that the rules contain the word 'analytic', which we do not understand! We understand what expressions the rules attribute analyticity to, but we do not understand what the rules attribute to those expressions. In short, before we can understand a rule which begins 'A statement S is analytic for language L_0 if and only if . . .', we must understand the general relative term 'analytic for'; we must understand 'S is analytic for L' where 'S' and 'L' are variables.

Alternatively we may, indeed, view the so-called rule as a conventional definition of a new simple symbol 'analytic-for-L_0', which might better be written untendentiously as 'K' so as not to seem to throw light on the interesting word 'analytic'. Obviously any number of classes K, M, N, etc. of statements of L_0 can be specified for various purposes or for no purpose; what does it mean to say that K, as against M, N, etc., is the class of the "analytic" statements of L_0?

By saying what statements are analytic for L_0 we explain 'analytic-for-L_0' but not 'analytic', not 'analytic for'. We do not begin to explain the idiom 'S is analytic for L' with variable

'*S*' and '*L*', even if we are content to limit the range of '*L*' to the realm of artificial languages.

Actually we do know enough about the intended significance of 'analytic' to know that analytic statements are supposed to be true. Let us then turn to a second form of semantical rule, which says not that such and such statements are analytic but simply that such and such statements are included among the truths. Such a rule is not subject to the criticism of containing the un-understood word 'analytic'; and we may grant for the sake of argument that there is no difficulty over the broader term 'true'. A semantical rule of this second type, a rule of truth, is not supposed to specify all the truths of the language; it merely stipulates, recursively or otherwise, a certain multitude of statements which, along with others unspecified, are to count as true. Such a rule may be conceded to be quite clear. Derivatively, afterward, analyticity can be demarcated thus: a statement is analytic if it is (not merely true but) true according to the semantical rule.

Still there is really no progress. Instead of appealing to an unexplained word 'analytic', we are now appealing to an unexplained phrase 'semantical rule'. Not every true statement which says that the statements of some class are true can count as a semantical rule—otherwise *all* truths would be "analytic" in the sense of being true according to semantical rules. Semantical rules are distinguishable, apparently, only by the fact of appearing on a page under the heading 'Semantical Rules'; and this heading is itself then meaningless.

We can say indeed that a statement is *analytic-for-L_0* if and only if it is true according to such and such specifically appended "semantical rules," but then we find ourselves back at essentially the same case which was originally discussed: '*S* is analytic-for-L_0 if and only if. . . .' Once we seek to explain '*S* is analytic for *L*' generally for variable '*L*' (even allowing limitation of '*L*' to artificial languages), the explanation 'true according to the semantical rules of *L*' is unavailing; for the relative term 'semantical rule of' is as much in need of clarification, at least, as 'analytic for'.

It may be instructive to compare the notion of semantical rule with that of postulate. Relative to a given set of postulates, it is easy to say what a postulate is: it is a member of the set. Relative to a given set of semantical rules, it is equally easy to say what a semantical rule is. But given simply a notation, mathematical or otherwise, and indeed as thoroughly understood a notation as you please in point of the translations or truth conditions of its statements, who can say which of its true statements rank as postulates? Obviously the question is meaningless—as meaningless as asking which points in Ohio are starting points. Any finite (or effectively specifiable infinite) selection of statements (preferably true ones, perhaps) is as much *a* set of postulates as any other. The word 'postulate' is significant only relative to an act of inquiry; we apply the word to a set of statements just in so far as we happen, for the year or the moment, to be thinking of those statements in relation to the statements which can be reached from them by some set of transformations to which we have seen fit to direct our attention. Now the notion of semantical rule is as sensible and meaningful as that of postulate, if conceived in a similarly relative spirit—relative, this time, to one or another particular enterprise of schooling unconversant persons in sufficient conditions for truth of statements of some natural or artificial language L. But from this point of view no one signalization of a subclass of the truths of L is intrinsically more a semantical rule than another; and, if 'analytic' means 'true by semantical rules', no one truth of L is analytic to the exclusion of another.[14]

It might conceivably be protested that an artificial language L (unlike a natural one) is a language in the ordinary sense *plus* a set of explicit semantical rules—the whole constituting, let us say, an ordered pair; and that the semantical rules of L then are specifiable simply as the second component of the pair L. But, by the same token and more simply, we might construe an artificial language L outright as an ordered pair whose second

[14] The foregoing paragraph was not part of the present essay as originally published. It was prompted by Martin (see Bibliography), as was the end of Essay VII.

component is the class of its analytic statements; and then the analytic statements of L become specifiable simply as the statements in the second component of L. Or better still, we might just stop tugging at our bootstraps altogether.

Not all the explanations of analyticity known to Carnap and his readers have been covered explicitly in the above considerations, but the extension to other forms is not hard to see. Just one additional factor should be mentioned which sometimes enters: sometimes the semantical rules are in effect rules of translation into ordinary language, in which case the analytic statements of the artificial language are in effect recognized as such from the analyticity of their specified translations in ordinary language. Here certainly there can be no thought of an illumination of the problem of analyticity from the side of the artificial language.

From the point of view of the problem of analyticity the notion of an artificial language with semantical rules is a *feu follet par excellence*. Semantical rules determining the analytic statements of an artificial language are of interest only in so far as we already understand the notion of analyticity; they are of no help in gaining this understanding.

Appeal to hypothetical languages of an artificially simple kind could conceivably be useful in clarifying analyticity, if the mental or behavioral or cultural factors relevant to analyticity—whatever they may be—were somehow sketched into the simplified model. But a model which takes analyticity merely as an irreducible character is unlikely to throw light on the problem of explicating analyticity.

It is obvious that truth in general depends on both language and extralinguistic fact. The statement 'Brutus killed Caesar' would be false if the world had been different in certain ways, but it would also be false if the word 'killed' happened rather to have the sense of 'begat'. Thus one is tempted to suppose in general that the truth of a statement is somehow analyzable into a linguistic component and a factual component. Given this supposition, it next seems reasonable that in some statements the factual component should be null; and these are the analytic statements. But, for all its a priori reasonableness, a boundary between analytic and synthetic statements simply has not been drawn. That there is such a distinction to be drawn at all is an unempirical dogma of empiricists, a metaphysical article of faith.

5. The Verification Theory and Reductionism

In the course of these somber reflections we have taken a dim view first of the notion of meaning, then of the notion of cognitive synonymy, and finally of the notion of analyticity. But what, it may be asked, of the verification theory of meaning? This phrase has established itself so firmly as a catchword of empiricism that we should be very unscientific indeed not to look beneath it for a possible key to the problem of meaning and the associated problems.

The verification theory of meaning, which has been conspicuous in the literature from Peirce onward, is that the meaning of a statement is the method of empirically confirming or infirming it. An analytic statement is that limiting case which is confirmed no matter what.

As urged in §1, we can as well pass over the question of meanings as entities and move straight to sameness of meaning, or synonymy. Then what the verification theory says is that statements are synonymous if and only if they are alike in point of method of empirical confirmation or infirmation.

This is an account of cognitive synonymy not of linguistic forms generally, but of statements.[15] However, from the concept of synonymy of statements we could derive the concept of synonymy for other linguistic forms, by considerations somewhat similar to those at the end of §3. Assuming the notion of "word," indeed, we could explain any two forms as synonymous when the

---

[15] The doctrine can indeed be formulated with terms rather than statements as the units. Thus Lewis describes the meaning of a term as "*a criterion in mind*, by reference to which one is able to apply or refuse to apply the expression in question in the case of presented, or imagined, things or situations" ([2], p. 133).—For an instructive account of the vicissitudes of the verification theory of meaning, centered however on the question of meaning*fulness* rather than synonymy and analyticity, see Hempel.

putting of the one form for an occurrence of the other in any statement (apart from occurrences within "words") yields a synonymous statement. Finally, given the concept of synonymy thus for linguistic forms generally, we could define analyticity in terms of synonymy and logical truth as in §1. For that matter, we could define analyticity more simply in terms of just synonymy of statements together with logical truth; it is not necessary to appeal to synonymy of linguistic forms other than statements. For a statement may be described as analytic simply when it is synonymous with a logically true statement.

So, if the verification theory can be accepted as an adequate account of statement synonymy, the notion of analyticity is saved after all. However, let us reflect. Statement synonymy is said to be likeness of method of empirical confirmation or infirmation. Just what are these methods which are to be compared for likeness? What, in other words, is the nature of the relation between a statement and the experiences which contribute to or detract from its confirmation?

The most naïve view of the relation is that it is one of direct report. This is *radical reductionism*. Every meaningful statement is held to be translatable into a statement (true or false) about immediate experience. Radical reductionism, in one form or another, well antedates the verification theory of meaning explicitly so called. Thus Locke and Hume held that every idea must either originate directly in sense experience or else be compounded of ideas thus originating; and taking a hint from Tooke we might rephrase this doctrine in semantical jargon by saying that a term, to be significant at all, must be either a name of a sense datum or a compound of such names or an abbreviation of such a compound. So stated, the doctrine remains ambiguous as between sense data as sensory events and sense data as sensory qualities; and it remains vague as to the admissible ways of compounding. Moreover, the doctrine is unnecessarily and intolerably restrictive in the term-by-term critique which it imposes. More reasonably, and without yet exceeding the limits of what I have called radical reductionism, we may take full statements as our significant units—thus demanding that our statements as wholes be translatable into sense-datum language, but not that they be translatable term by term.

This emendation would unquestionably have been welcome to Locke and Hume and Tooke, but historically it had to await an important reorientation in semantics—the reorientation whereby the primary vehicle of meaning came to be seen no longer in the term but in the statement. This reorientation, seen in Bentham and Frege, underlies Russell's concept of incomplete symbols defined in use;[16] also it is implicit in the verification theory of meaning, since the objects of verification are statements.

Radical reductionism, conceived now with statements as units, set itself the task of specifying a sense-datum language and showing how to translate the rest of significant discourse, statement by statement, into it. Carnap embarked on this project in the *Aufbau*.

The language which Carnap adopted as his starting point was not a sense-datum language in the narrowest conceivable sense, for it included also the notations of logic, up through higher set theory. In effect it included the whole language of pure mathematics. The ontology implicit in it (that is, the range of values of its variables) embraced not only sensory events but classes, classes of classes, and so on. Empiricists there are who would boggle at such prodigality. Carnap's starting point is very parsimonious, however, in its extralogical or sensory part. In a series of constructions in which he exploits the resources of modern logic with much ingenuity, Carnap succeeds in defining a wide array of important additional sensory concepts which, but for his constructions, one would not have dreamed were definable on so slender a basis. He was the first empiricist who, not content with asserting the reducibility of science to terms of immediate experience, took serious steps toward carrying out the reduction.

If Carnap's starting point is satisfactory, still his construc-

---

[16] See above, p. 6.

tions were, as he himself stressed, only a fragment of the full program. The construction of even the simplest statements about the physical world was left in a sketchy state. Carnap's suggestions on this subject were, despite their sketchiness, very suggestive. He explained spatio-temporal point-instants as quadruples of real numbers and envisaged assignment of sense qualities to point-instants according to certain canons. Roughly summarized, the plan was that qualities should be assigned to point-instants in such a way as to achieve the laziest world compatible with our experience. The principle of least action was to be our guide in constructing a world from experience.

Carnap did not seem to recognize, however, that his treatment of physical objects fell short of reduction not merely through sketchiness, but in principle. Statements of the form 'Quality q is at point-instant $x;y;z;t$' were, according to his canons, to be apportioned truth values in such a way as to maximize and minimize certain over-all features, and with growth of experience the truth values were to be progressively revised in the same spirit. I think this is a good schematization (deliberately oversimplified, to be sure) of what science really does; but it provides no indication, not even the sketchiest, of how a statement of the form 'Quality q is at $x;y;z;t$' could ever be translated into Carnap's initial language of sense data and logic. The connective 'is at' remains an added undefined connective; the canons counsel us in its use but not in its elimination.

Carnap seems to have appreciated this point afterward; for in his later writings he abandoned all notion of the translatability of statements about the physical world into statements about immediate experience. Reductionism in its radical form has long since ceased to figure in Carnap's philosophy.

But the dogma of reductionism has, in a subtler and more tenuous form, continued to influence the thought of empiricists. The notion lingers that to each statement, or each synthetic statement, there is associated a unique range of possible sensory events such that the occurrence of any of them would add to the likelihood of truth of the statement, and that there is associated also another unique range of possible sensory events whose occurrence would detract from that likelihood. This notion is of course implicit in the verification theory of meaning.

The dogma of reductionism survives in the supposition that each statement, taken in isolation from its fellows, can admit of confirmation or infirmation at all. My countersuggestion, issuing essentially from Carnap's doctrine of the physical world in the *Aufbau*, is that our statements about the external world face the tribunal of sense experience not individually but only as a corporate body.[17]

The dogma of reductionism, even in its attenuated form, is intimately connected with the other dogma—that there is a cleavage between the analytic and the synthetic. We have found ourselves led, indeed, from the latter problem to the former through the verification theory of meaning. More directly, the one dogma clearly supports the other in this way: as long as it is taken to be significant in general to speak of the confirmation and infirmation of a statement, it seems significant to speak also of a limiting kind of statement which is vacuously confirmed, *ipso facto*, come what may; and such a statement is analytic.

The two dogmas are, indeed, at root identical. We lately reflected that in general the truth of statements does obviously depend both upon language and upon extralinguistic fact; and we noted that this obvious circumstance carries in its train, not logically but all too naturally, a feeling that the truth of a statement is somehow analyzable into a linguistic component and a factual component. The factual component must, if we are empiricists, boil down to a range of confirmatory experiences. In the extreme case where the linguistic component is all that matters, a true statement is analytic. But I hope we are now impressed with how stubbornly the distinction between analytic and synthetic has resisted any straightforward drawing. I am impressed also, apart from prefabricated examples of black and white balls in an urn, with how baffling the problem has always

[17] This doctrine was well argued by Duhem, pp. 303–328. Or see Lowinger, pp. 132–140.

been of arriving at any explicit theory of the empirical confirmation of a synthetic statement. My present suggestion is that it is nonsense, and the root of much nonsense, to speak of a linguistic component and a factual component in the truth of any individual statement. Taken collectively, science has its double dependence upon language and experience; but this duality is not significantly traceable into the statements of science taken one by one.

The idea of defining a symbol in use was, as remarked, an advance over the impossible term-by-term empiricism of Locke and Hume. The statement, rather than the term, came with Bentham to be recognized as the unit accountable to an empiricist critique. But what I am now urging is that even in taking the statement as unit we have drawn our grid too finely. The unit of empirical significance is the whole of science.

6. Empiricism without the Dogmas

The totality of our so-called knowledge or beliefs, from the most casual matters of geography and history to the profoundest laws of atomic physics or even of pure mathematics and logic, is a man-made fabric which impinges on experience only along the edges. Or, to change the figure, total science is like a field of force whose boundary conditions are experience. A conflict with experience at the periphery occasions readjustments in the interior of the field. Truth values have to be redistributed over some of our statements. Reëvaluation of some statements entails reëvaluation of others, because of their logical interconnections —the logical laws being in turn simply certain further statements of the system, certain further elements of the field. Having reëvaluated one statement we must reëvaluate some others, which may be statements logically connected with the first or may be the statements of logical connections themselves. But the total field is so underdetermined by its boundary conditions, experience, that there is much latitude of choice as to what statements to reëvaluate in the light of any single contrary experience. No particular experiences are linked with any particular statements in the interior of the field, except indirectly through considerations of equilibrium affecting the field as a whole.

If this view is right, it is misleading to speak of the empirical content of an individual statement—especially if it is a statement at all remote from the experiential periphery of the field. Furthermore it becomes folly to seek a boundary between synthetic statements, which hold contingently on experience, and analytic statements, which hold come what may. Any statement can be held true come what may, if we make drastic enough adjustments elsewhere in the system. Even a statement very close to the periphery can be held true in the face of recalcitrant experience by pleading hallucination or by amending certain statements of the kind called logical laws. Conversely, by the same token, no statement is immune to revision. Revision even of the logical law of the excluded middle has been proposed as a means of simplifying quantum mechanics; and what difference is there in principle between such a shift and the shift whereby Kepler superseded Ptolemy, or Einstein Newton, or Darwin Aristotle?

For vividness I have been speaking in terms of varying distances from a sensory periphery. Let me try now to clarify this notion without metaphor. Certain statements, though *about* physical objects and not sense experience, seem peculiarly germane to sense experience—and in a selective way: some statements to some experiences, others to others. Such statements, especially germane to particular experiences, I picture as near the periphery. But in this relation of "germaneness" I envisage nothing more than a loose association reflecting the relative likelihood, in practice, of our choosing one statement rather than another for revision in the event of recalcitrant experience. For example, we can imagine recalcitrant experiences to which we would surely be inclined to accommodate our system by reëvaluating just the statement that there are brick houses on Elm Street, together with related statements on the same topic. We can imagine other recalcitrant experiences to which we would be inclined to accommodate our system by reëvaluating just the statement that there are no centaurs, along with kindred statements. A recalcitrant experience can, I have urged, be accommodated by any of various alternative reëvaluations in various alternative quarters of the total system; but, in the cases which we are now imagining, our natural tendency to disturb the total system as little as possible would lead us to focus our revisions upon these specific statements concerning brick houses or centaurs. These statements are felt, therefore, to have a sharper empirical reference than highly theoretical statements of physics or logic or ontology. The latter statements may be thought of as relatively centrally located within the total network, meaning merely that little preferential connection with any particular sense data obtrudes itself.

As an empiricist I continue to think of the conceptual scheme of science as a tool, ultimately, for predicting future experience in the light of past experience. Physical objects are conceptually imported into the situation as convenient intermediaries—not by definition in terms of experience, but simply as irreducible posits[18] comparable, epistemologically, to the gods of Homer. For my part I do, qua lay physicist, believe in physical objects and not in Homer's gods; and I consider it a scientific error to believe otherwise. But in point of epistemological footing the physical objects and the gods differ only in degree and not in kind. Both sorts of entities enter our conception only as cultural posits. The myth of physical objects is epistemologically superior to most in that it has proved more efficacious than other myths as a device for working a manageable structure into the flux of experience.

Positing does not stop with macroscopic physical objects. Objects at the atomic level are posited to make the laws of macroscopic objects, and ultimately the laws of experience, simpler and more manageable; and we need not expect or demand full definition of atomic and subatomic entities in terms of macroscopic ones, any more than definition of macroscopic

[18] Cf. pp. 17f above.

things in terms of sense data. Science is a continuation of common sense, and it continues the common-sense expedient of swelling ontology to simplify theory.

Physical objects, small and large, are not the only posits. Forces are another example; and indeed we are told nowadays that the boundary between energy and matter is obsolete. Moreover, the abstract entities which are the substance of mathematics—ultimately classes and classes of classes and so on up—are another posit in the same spirit. Epistemologically these are myths on the same footing with physical objects and gods, neither better nor worse except for differences in the degree to which they expedite our dealings with sense experiences.

The over-all algebra of rational and irrational numbers is underdetermined by the algebra of rational numbers, but is smoother and more convenient; and it includes the algebra of rational numbers as a jagged or gerrymandered part.[19] Total science, mathematical and natural and human, is similarly but more extremely underdetermined by experience. The edge of the system must be kept squared with experience; the rest, with all its elaborate myths or fictions, has as its objective the simplicity of laws.

Ontological questions, under this view, are on a par with questions of natural science.[20] Consider the question whether to countenance classes as entities. This, as I have argued elsewhere,[21] is the question whether to quantify with respect to variables which take classes as values. Now Carnap [6] has maintained that this is a question not of matters of fact but of choosing a convenient language form, a convenient conceptual scheme or framework for science. With this I agree, but only on the proviso that the same be conceded regarding scientific hypotheses generally. Carnap ([6], p. 32n) has recognized that he is able to preserve a double standard for ontological questions and scientific hypotheses only by assuming an absolute distinc-

---

[19] Cf. p. 18 above.
[20] "L'ontologie fait corps avec la science elle-même et ne peut en être separée." Meyerson, p. 439.
[21] Above, pp. 12f; below, pp. 102ff.

tion between the analytic and the synthetic; and I need not say again that this is a distinction which I reject.[22]

The issue over there being classes seems more a question of convenient conceptual scheme; the issue over there being centaurs, or brick houses on Elm Street, seems more a question of fact. But I have been urging that this difference is only one of degree, and that it turns upon our vaguely pragmatic inclination to adjust one strand of the fabric of science rather than another in accommodating some particular recalcitrant experience. Conservatism figures in such choices, and so does the quest for simplicity.

Carnap, Lewis, and others take a pragmatic stand on the question of choosing between language forms, scientific frameworks; but their pragmatism leaves off at the imagined boundary between the analytic and the synthetic. In repudiating such a boundary I espouse a more thorough pragmatism. Each man is given a scientific heritage plus a continuing barrage of sensory stimulation; and the considerations which guide him in warping his scientific heritage to fit his continuing sensory promptings are, where rational, pragmatic.

[22] For an effective expression of further misgivings over this distinction, see White [2].

III

THE PROBLEM OF MEANING
IN LINGUISTICS

1

Lexicography is concerned, or seems to be concerned, with identification of meanings, and the investigation of semantic change is concerned with change of meaning. Pending a satisfactory explanation of the notion of meaning, linguists in semantic fields are in the situation of not knowing what they are talking about. This is not an untenable situation. Ancient astronomers knew the movements of the planets remarkably well without knowing what sort of things the planets were. But it is a theoretically unsatisfactory situation, as the more theoretically minded among the linguists are painfully aware.

Confusion of meaning with reference[1] has encouraged a tendency to take the notion of meaning for granted. It is felt that the meaning of the word 'man' is as tangible as our neighbor and that the meaning of the phrase 'Evening Star' is as clear as the star in the sky. And it is felt that to question or repudiate the notion of meaning is to suppose a world in which there is just language and nothing for language to refer to. Actually we can acknowledge a worldful of objects, and let our singular and general terms refer to those objects in their several ways to our hearts' content, without ever taking up the topic of meaning.

An object referred to, named by a singular term or denoted by a general term, can be anything under the sun. Meanings, however, purport to be entities of a special sort: the meaning of

[1] See above, pp. 9, 21f.

an expression is the idea expressed. Now there is considerable agreement among modern linguists that the idea of an idea, the idea of the mental counterpart of a linguistic form, is worse than worthless for linguistic science. I think the behaviorists are right in holding that talk of ideas is bad business even for psychology. The evil of the idea idea is that its use, like the appeal in Molière to a *virtus dormitiva*, engenders an illusion of having explained something. And the illusion is increased by the fact that things wind up in a vague enough state to insure a certain stability, or freedom from further progress.

Let us then look back to the lexicographer, supposed as he is to be concerned with meanings, and see what he is really trafficking in if not in mental entities. The answer is not far to seek: the lexicographer, like any linguist, studies linguistic forms. He differs from the so-called formal linguist only in that he is concerned to correlate linguistic forms with one another in his own special way, namely, synonyms with synonyms. The characteristic feature of semantical parts of linguistics, notably lexicography, comes to be not that there is an appeal to meanings but that there is a concern with synonymy.

What happens in this maneuver is that we fix on one important context of the baffling word 'meaning', namely the context '*alike in* meaning', and resolve to treat this whole context in the spirit of a single word 'synonymous', thus not being tempted to seek meanings as intermediary entities. But, even supposing that the notion of synonymy can eventually be provided with a satisfactory criterion, still this maneuver only takes care of the one context of the word 'meaning'—the context 'alike in meaning'. Does the word also have other contexts that should concern linguists? Yes, there is certainly one more—the context 'having meaning'. Here a parallel maneuver is in order: treat the context 'having meaning' in the spirit of a single word, 'significant', and continue to turn our backs on the supposititious entities called meanings.

Significance is the trait with respect to which the subject matter of linguistics is studied by the grammarian. The grammarian catalogues short forms and works out the laws of their concatenation, and the end product of this is no more nor less than a specification of the class of all possible linguistic forms, simple and composite, of the language under investigation—the class of all significant sequences, if we accept a liberal standard of significance. The lexicographer, on the other hand, is concerned not with specifying the class of significant sequences for the given language, but rather with specifying the class of pairs of mutually synonymous sequences for the given language or, perhaps, pair of languages. The grammarian and the lexicographer are concerned with meaning to an equal degree, be it zero or otherwise; the grammarian wants to know what forms are significant, or *have* meaning, while the lexicographer wants to know what forms are synonymous, or *alike* in meaning. If it is urged that the grammarian's notion of significant sequences should not be viewed as resting on a prior notion of meaning, I applaud; and I say the lexicographer's notion of synonymy is entitled to the same compliment. What had been the problem of meaning boils down now to a pair of problems in which meaning is best not mentioned; one is the problem of making sense of the notion of significant sequence, and the other is the problem of making sense of the notion of synonymy. What I want to emphasize is that the lexicographer had no monopoly on the problem of meaning. The problem of significant sequence and the problem of synonymy are twin offspring of the problem of meaning.

2

Let us suppose that our grammarian is at work on a hitherto unstudied language, and that his own contact with the language has been limited to his field work. As grammarian he is concerned to discover the bounds of the class K of significant sequences of the language. Synonymy correlations of members of K with English sequences and with one another are not his business; they are the business of the lexicographer.

There is presumably no upper limit to the lengths of members of K. Moreover, parts of significant sequences count as significant, down to the smallest adopted units of analysis; so such units, whatever they are, are the shortest members of K. Besides the length dimension, however, there is a dimension of thickness to consider. For, given two utterances of equal and arbitrary length and fairly similar acoustical make-up, we must know whether to count them as occurrences of two slightly different members of K or as two slightly different occurrences of one and the same member of K. The question of thickness is the question what acoustical differences to count as relevant and what ones to count merely as inconsequential idiosyncrasies of voice and accent.

The question of thickness is settled by cataloguing the *phonemes*—the single sounds, distinguished as coarsely as possible for purposes of the language. Two subtly differing sounds count as the same phoneme unless it is possible, by putting one for the other in some utterance, to change the meaning of the utterance.[2] Now the notion of phoneme, thus formulated, depends obviously and notoriously on the notion of sameness of meaning, or synonymy. Our grammarian, if he is to remain pure grammarian and eschew lexicography, must carry out his program of delimiting K without the help of a notion of phoneme so defined.

There seems indeed, at first glance, to be an easy way out: he can simply enumerate the phonemes needed for the particular language at hand, and dispense with the general notion of phoneme defined in terms of synonymy. This expedient would be quite admissible as a mere technical aid to solving the grammarian's problem of specifying the membership of K, if the problem of specifying the membership of K could itself be *posed* without prior appeal to the general notion of phoneme. But the fact is otherwise. The class K which it is the grammarian's empirical business to describe is a class of sequences of phonemes, and each phoneme is a class of brief events. (It will be convenient to swallow this much platonism for present purposes, though some logical maneuvers might serve to reduce it.) The grammarian's problem is in part objectively set for him thus: every speech event which he encounters in his field work

[2] Cf. Bloch and Trager, pp. 38–52, or Bloomfield, pp. 74–92.

counts as a sample of a member of K. But the delimiting of the several members of K, that is, the grouping of mutually resemblant acoustical histories into bundles of proper thickness to qualify as linguistic forms, needs also to have some objective significance if the task of the field grammarian is to be made sense of as an empirical and objective task at all. This need is fulfilled if the general notion of phoneme is at hand, as a general relative term: 'x is a phoneme for language L', with variable 'x' and 'L', or 'x is a phoneme for speaker s', with variable 'x' and 's'. Thereupon the grammarian's business, with respect to a language L, can be stated as the business of finding what sequences of phonemes of L are significant for L. Statement of the grammarian's purpose thus depends not only on 'significant', as we had been prepared to expect, but also on 'phoneme'.

But we might still seek to free grammar of dependence on the notion of synonymy, by somehow freeing the notion of phoneme itself of such dependence. It has been conjectured, for example, by Bühler, that this might in principle be accomplished. Let the continuum of sounds be arranged in acoustical or physiological order in one or more dimensions, say two, and plotted against frequency of occurrence, so that we come out with a three-dimensional relief map in which altitude represents frequency of occurrence. Then it is suggested that the major humps correspond to the phonemes. There are abundant reasons to suspect that neither this oversimplified account nor anything remotely resembling it can possibly provide an adequate definition of the phoneme; and phonologists have not neglected to adduce such reasons. As a means of isolating other points of comparison between grammar and lexicography, however, let us make the unrealistic assumption that our grammarian has some such nonsemantical definition of phoneme. Then his remaining task is to devise a recursive description of a class K of forms which will comprise all and only those sequences of phonemes which are in fact significant.

The basic point of view is that the class K is objectively determinate before the grammatical research is begun; it is the class of the significant sequences, the sequences capable of occurring in the normal stream of speech (supposing for the moment that this terminology is itself significant). But the grammarian wants to reproduce this same class in other terms, formal terms; he wants to devise, in terms of elaborate conditions of phoneme succession alone, a necessary and sufficient condition for membership in K. He is an empirical scientist, and his result will be right or wrong according as he reproduces that objectively predetermined class K or some other.

Our grammarian's attempted recursive specification of K will follow the orthodox line, we may suppose, of listing "morphemes" and describing constructions. Morphemes, according to the books,[3] are the significant forms which are not resoluble into shorter significant forms. They comprise affixes, word stems, and whole words in so far as these are not analyzable into subsidiary morphemes. But we can spare our grammarian any general problem of defining morpheme by allowing him simply to list his so-called morphemes exhaustively. They become simply a convenient segmentation of heard phoneme sequences, chopped out as convenient building blocks for his purpose. He frames his constructions in the simplest way that will enable him to generate all members of K from his morphemes, and he cuts his morphemes to allow for the simplest constructions. Morphemes, like higher units such as might be called words or free forms, may thus be viewed simply as intermediate stages in a process which, over all, is still describable as reproduction of K in terms of conditions of phoneme succession.

There is no denying that the grammarian's reproduction of K, as I have schematized it, is purely formal, that is, free of semantics. But the setting of the grammarian's problem is quite another matter, for it turns on a prior notion of significant sequence, or possible normal utterance. Without this notion, or something to somewhat the same effect, we cannot say what the grammarian is trying to do—what he is trying to match in his formal reproduction of K—nor wherein the rightness or wrongness of his results might consist. We are thus squarely

---

[3] Bloch and Trager, p. 54; Bloomfield, pp. 161–168.

confronted with one of the twin offspring of the problem of meaning, namely, the problem of defining the general notion of significant sequence.

3

It is not satisfactory to say that a significant sequence is simply any sequence of phonemes uttered by any of the *Naturkinder* of our grammarian's chosen valley. What are wanted as significant sequences include not just those uttered but also those which *could* be uttered without reactions suggesting bizarreness of idiom. The joker here is 'could'; we cannot substitute 'will'. The significant sequences, being subject to no length limit, are infinite in variety; whereas, from the dawn of the language under investigation to the time when it will have evolved to the point where our grammarian would disown it, only a finite sample of this infinite manifold will have been uttered.

The desired class K of significant sequences is the culmination of a series of four classes of increasing magnitude, H, I, J, and K, as follows. H is the class of observed sequences, excluding any which are ruled inappropriate in the sense of being nonlinguistic or belonging to alien dialects. I is the class of all such observed sequences and all that ever will happen to be professionally observed, excluding again those which are ruled inappropriate. J is the class of all sequences ever occurring, now or in the past or future, within or without professional observation—excluding, again, only those which are ruled inappropriate. K, finally, is the infinite class of all those sequences, with exclusion of the inappropriate ones as usual, which *could* be uttered without bizarreness reactions. K is the class which the grammarian wants to approximate in his formal reconstruction, and K is more inclusive even than J, let alone H and I. Now the class H is a matter of finished record; the class I is, or could be, a matter of growing record; the class J goes beyond any record, but still has a certain common-sense reality; but not even this can very confidently be said of K, because of the 'could'.

I expect we must leave the 'could' unreduced. It has some

operational import, indeed, but only in a partial way. It does require our grammarian to bring into his formal reconstruction of K all of the actually observed cases, that is, all of H. Further, it commits him to the prediction that all cases to be observed in the future will conform, that is, all of I belongs in K. Further still, it commits him to the scientific hypothesis that all unobserved cases fall in this K, that is, all of J. Now what more does the 'could' cover? What is the rationale behind that infinite additional membership of K, over and above the finite part J? This vast supplementary force of 'could', in the present instance and elsewhere, is perhaps a vestige of Indo-European myth, fossilized in the subjunctive mood.

What our grammarian does is evident enough. He frames his formal reconstruction of K along the grammatically simplest lines he can, compatibly with inclusion of H, plausibility of the predicted inclusion of I, plausibility of the hypothesis of inclusion of J, and plausibility, further, of the exclusion of all sequences which ever actually do bring bizarreness reactions. Our basis for saying what 'could' be generally consists, I suggest, in what *is* plus *simplicity* of the laws whereby we describe and extrapolate what is. I see no more objective way of construing the *conditio irrealis*.

Concerning the notion of significant sequence, one of the two survivals of the notion of meaning, we have now observed the following. It is needed in setting the grammarian's task. But it is describable, without appeal to meanings as such, as denoting any sequence which could be uttered in the society under consideration without reactions suggesting bizarreness of idiom. This notion of a reaction suggesting bizarreness of idiom would want some refinement eventually. A considerable problem of refinement is involved also in the preliminary putting aside of so-called nonlinguistic noises, as well as utterances in alien dialects. Also there is the general methodological problem, of a pretty philosophical kind, which is raised by the word 'could'. This is a problem common to concept-building in most subjects (apart from logic and mathematics, where it happens to be well cleared up); I have outlined one attitude toward it.

We should also remind ourselves of the oversimplification which I made with regard to morphemes, when I treated them merely as convenient phoneme sequences which our grammarian specifies by enumeration in the course of his formal reconstruction of the class of significant sequences from the phonemes. This is unrealistic because it requires our grammarian to exhaust the vocabulary, instead of allowing him to leave certain open categories, comparable to our nouns and verbs, subject to enrichment *ad libitum*. Now if on the other hand we allow him some open morpheme categories, his reconstruction of the class *K* of significant sequences ceases to be a formal construction from phonemes; the most we can say for it is that it is a formal reconstruction from phonemes and his open morpheme categories. So the problem remains how he is going to characterize his open morpheme categories—since enumeration no longer serves. This gap must be watched for possible intrusion of an unanalyzed semantical element.

I do not want to take leave of the topic of significant sequence without mentioning one curious further problem which the notion raises. I shall speak now of English rather than a hypothetical heathen tongue. Any nonsensical and thoroughly un-English string of sounds can occur within a perfectly intelligible English sentence, even a true one, if in effect we quote the nonsense and say in the rest of our sentence that the quoted matter *is* nonsense, or is not English, or consists of four syllables, or rimes with 'Kalamazoo', etc. If the whole inclusive sentence is to be called normal English speech, then the rubbish inside it has occurred in normal English speech, and we have thus lost the means of excluding any pronounceable sequence from the category of significant sequence. Thus we must either narrow our concept of normality to exclude, for present purposes, sentences which use quotation, or else we must narrow our concept of occurrence to exclude occurrence within quotation. In either event we have the problem of identifying the spoken analogue of quotation marks, and of doing so in general enough terms so that our concept of significant sequence will not be limited in advance to some one preconceived language such as English.

In any case we have seen that the problem of significant sequence admits of considerable fragmentation; and this is one of the two aspects into which the problem of meaning seemed to resolve, namely, the aspect of the having of meaning. The fact that this aspect of the problem of meaning is in such halfway tolerable shape accounts, no doubt, for the tendency to think of grammar as a formal, nonsemantical part of linguistics. Let us turn now to the other and more forbidding aspect of the problem of meaning, that of likeness in meaning, or synonymy.

4

A lexicographer may be concerned with synonymy between forms in one language and forms in another or, as in compiling a domestic dictionary, he may be concerned with synonymy between forms in the same language. It is an open question how satisfactorily the two cases can be subsumed under a single general formulation of the synonymy concept, for it is an open question whether the synonymy concept can be satisfactorily clarified for either case. Let us first limit our attention to synonymy within a language.

So-called substitution criteria, or conditions of interchangeability, have in one form or another played central rôles in modern grammar. For the synonymy problem of semantics such an approach seems more obvious still. However, the notion of the interchangeability of two linguistic forms makes sense only in so far as answers are provided to these two questions: (a) In just what sorts of contextual position, if not in all, are the two forms to be interchangeable? (b) The forms are to be interchangeable *salvo quo*? Supplanting one form by another in any context changes something, namely, form at least; and (b) asks what feature the interchange is to leave invariant. Alternative answers to (a) and (b) give alternative notions of interchangeability, some suited to defining grammatical correspondences and others, conceivably, to defining synonymy.

In §3 of Essay II we tried answering (b), for purposes of synonymy, with *veritate*. We found that something had still to be done about (a), in view, for example, of the difficulty presented by quotation. So we answered (a), lamely appealing to a prior conception of "word." Then we found that interchangeability *salva veritate* was too weak a condition for synonymy if the language as a whole was "extensional," and that in other languages it was an unilluminating condition, involving something like a vicious circle.

It is not clear that the problem of synonymy discussed in those pages is the same as the lexicographer's problem. For in those pages we were concerned with "cognitive" synonymy, which abstracts from much that the lexicographer would want to preserve in his translations and paraphrases. Even the lexicographer is indeed ready to equate, as synonymous, many forms which differ perceptibly in imaginative associations and poetic value;[4] but the optimum sense of synonymy for his purpose is probably narrower than synonymy in the supposed cognitive sense. However this may be, certainly the negative findings which were summed up in the preceding paragraph carry over; the lexicographer cannot answer (b) with *veritate*. The interchangeability which he seeks in synonymy must not merely be such as to assure that true statements remain true, and false ones false, when synonyms are substituted within them; it must assure further that statements go over into statements with which they as wholes are somehow synonymous.

This last observation does not recommend itself as a definition, because of its circularity: forms are synonymous when their interchange leaves their contexts synonymous. But it has the virtue of hinting that substitution is not the main point, and that what we need in the first place is some notion of synonymy for long segments of discourse. The hint is opportune; for, independently of the foregoing considerations, three reasons can be adduced for approaching the problem of synonymy from the point of view of long segments of discourse.

First, any interchangeability criterion for synonymy of short

[4] See above, p. 28.

forms would obviously be limited to synonymy within a language; otherwise interchange would produce polyglot jumbles. *Inter*linguistic synonymy must be a relation, primarily, between segments of discourse which are long enough to bear consideration in abstraction from a containing context peculiar to one or the other particular language. I say "primarily" because interlinguistic synonymy might indeed be denned for the component forms afterward in some derivative way.

Second, a retreat to longer segments tends to overcome the difficulty of ambiguity or homonymy. Homonymy gets in the way of the law that if a is synonymous with b and b with c, then a is synonymous with c. For, if b has two meanings (to revert to the ordinary parlance of meanings), a may be synonymous with b in one sense of b and b with c in the other sense of b. This difficulty is sometimes dealt with by treating an ambiguous form as two forms, but this expedient has the drawback of making the concept of form depend on that of synonymy.

Third, there is the circumstance that in glossing a word we have so frequently to content ourselves with a lame partial synonym plus stage directions. Thus in glossing 'addled' we say 'spoiled' and add 'said of an egg'. This widespread circumstance reflects the fact that synonymy in the small is no primary concern of the lexicographer; lame synonyms plus stage directions are quite satisfactory in so far as they expedite his primary business of explaining how to translate or paraphrase long speeches. We may continue to characterize the lexicographer's domain squarely as synonymy, but only by recognizing synonymy as primarily a relation of sufficiently long segments of discourse.

So we may view the lexicographer as interested, ultimately, only in cataloguing synonym pairs which are sequences of sufficient length to admit of synonymy in some primary sense. Naturally he cannot catalogue these true synonym pairs directly, in any exhaustive way, because they are altogether limitless in number and variety. His case is parallel to that of the grammarian, who for the same reason was unable to catalogue the significant sequences directly. The grammarian accomplished his end indirectly, by fixing on a class of atomic units capable of enumeration and then propounding rules for compounding them to get all significant sequences. Similarly the lexicographer accomplishes his end indirectly, the end of specifying the infinitely numerous genuine pairs of long synonyms; and this he does by fixing on a class of short forms capable of enumeration and then explaining as systematically as he can how to construct genuine synonyms for all sufficiently long forms compounded of those short ones. These short forms are in effect the word entries in his glossary, and the explanations of how to construct genuine synonyms of all sufficiently long compounds are what appear as the glosses in his glossary, typically a mixture of quasi synonyms and stage directions.

Thus the lexicographer's actual activity, his glossing of short forms by appeal to quasi synonyms and stage directions, is not antithetical to his being concerned purely and simply with genuine synonymy on the part of forms sufficiently long to admit of genuine synonymy. Something like his actual activity is indeed the only possible way of cataloguing, in effect, the limitless class of pairs of genuinely synonymous longer forms.

I exploited just now a parallelism between the grammarian's indirect reconstruction of the limitless class of significant sequences and the lexicographer's indirect reconstruction of the limitless class of genuine synonym pairs. This parallelism bears further exploiting. It brings out that the lexicographer's reconstruction of the class of synonym pairs is just as formal in spirit as the grammarian's reconstruction of the class of significant sequences. The invidious use of the word 'formal', to favor grammar as against lexicography, is thus misleading. Both the lexicographer and the grammarian would simply list the membership of the respective classes in which they are interested, were it not for the vastness, the infinitude even, of the numbers involved. On the other hand, just as the grammarian needs over and above his formal constructions a prior notion of significant sequence for the setting of his problem, so the lexicographer needs a prior notion of synonymy for the setting of his. In the setting of their problems, the grammarian and the lexicographer draw equally on our heritage from the old notion of meaning.

It is clear from the foregoing reflections that the notion of synonymy needed in the statement of the lexicographer's problem is synonymy only as between sequences which are long enough to be pretty clean-cut about their synonymy connections. But in conclusion I want to stress what a baffling problem this remaining problem of synonymy, even relatively clean-cut and well-behaved synonymy, is.

5

Synonymy of two forms is supposed vaguely to consist in an approximate likeness in the situations which evoke the two forms, and an approximate likeness in the effect of either form on the hearer. For simplicity let us forget this second requirement and concentrate on the first—the likeness of situations. What I have to say from here on will be so vague, at best, that this further inaccuracy will not much matter.

As everyone is quick to point out, no two situations are quite alike; situations in which even the same form is uttered are unlike in myriad ways. What matters rather is likeness in *relevant respects*. Now the problem of finding the relevant respects is, if we think of the matter in a sufficiently oversimplified way, a problem typical of empirical science. We observe a speaker of Kalaba, say—to adopt Pike's myth—and we look for correlations or so-called causal connections between the noises he makes and the other things that are observed to be happening. As in any empirical search for correlations or so-called causal connections, we guess at the relevance of one or another feature and then try by further observation, or even experiment, to confirm or refute our hypothesis. Actually, in lexicography this guessing at possible relevances is expedited by our natural familiarity with the basic lines of human interest. Finally, having found fair evidence for correlating a given Kalaba sound sequence with a given combination of circumstances, we conjecture synonymy of that sound sequence with another, in English, say, which is correlated with the same circumstances.

As I unnecessarily remarked, this account is oversimplified. Now I want to stress one serious respect in which it is oversimplified: the relevant features of the situation issuing in a given Kalaba utterance are in large part concealed in the person of the speaker, where they were implanted by his earlier environment. This concealment is partly good, for our purposes, and partly bad. It is good in so far as it isolates the subject's narrowly linguistic training. If we could assume that our Kalaba speaker and our English speaker, when observed in like external situations, differed only in how they say things and not in *what* they say, so to speak, then the methodology of synonymy determinations would be pretty smooth; the narrowly linguistic part of the causal complex, different for the two speakers, would be conveniently out of sight, while all the parts of the causal complex decisive of synonymy or heteronymy were open to observation. But of course the trouble is that not only the narrowly linguistic habits of vocabulary and syntax are imported by each speaker from his unknown past.

The difficulty here is not just that those subjective components of the situation are hard to ferret out. This difficulty, if it were all, would make for practical uncertainty and frequent error in lexicographical pronouncements, but it would be irrelevant to the problem of a theoretical definition of synonymy— irrelevant, that is, to the problem of coherently stating the lexicographer's purpose. Theoretically the more important difficulty is that, as Cassirer and Whorf have stressed, there is in principle no separating language from the rest of the world, at least as conceived by the speaker. Basic differences in language are bound up, as likely as not, with differences in the way in which the speakers articulate the world itself into things and properties, time and space, elements, forces, spirits, and so on. It is not clear even in principle that it makes sense to think of words and syntax as varying from language to language while the content stays fixed; yet precisely this fiction is involved in speaking of synonymy, at least as between expressions of radically different languages.

What provides the lexicographer with an entering wedge is

the fact that there are many basic features of men's ways of conceptualizing their environment, of breaking the world down into things, which are common to all cultures. Every man is likely to see an apple or breadfruit or rabbit first and foremost as a unitary whole rather than as a congeries of smaller units or as a fragment of a larger environment, though from a sophisticated point of view all these attitudes are tenable. Every man will tend to segregate a mass of moving matter as a unit, separate from the static background, and to pay it particular attention. Again there are conspicuous phenomena of weather which one man may be expected to endow with much the same conceptual boundaries as another; and similarly perhaps for some basic internal states such as hunger. As long as we adhere to this presumably common fund of conceptualization, we can successfully proceed on the working assumption that our Kalaba speaker and our English speaker, observed in like external situations, differ only in how they say things and not in what they say.

The nature of this entering wedge into a strange lexicon encourages the misconception of meaning as reference, since words at this stage are construed, typically, by pointing to the object referred to. So it may not be amiss to remind ourselves that meaning is not reference even here. The reference might be the Evening Star, to return to Frege's example, and hence also the Morning Star, which is the same thing; but 'Evening Star' might nevertheless be a good translation and 'Morning Star' a bad one.

I have suggested that our lexicographer's obvious first moves in picking up some initial Kalaba vocabulary are at bottom a matter of exploiting the overlap of our cultures. From this nucleus he works outward, ever more fallibly and conjecturally, by a series of clues and hunches. Thus he begins with a fund of correlations of Kalaba sentences with English sentences at the level where our cultures meet. Most of these sentences classify conspicuously segregated objects. Then he breaks these Kalaba sentences down into short component elements, and makes tentative English translations of these elements, compatible with his initial sentence translations. On this basis, he frames hypotheses as to the English translations of new combinations of those elements—combinations which as wholes have not been translated in the direct way. He tests his hypotheses as best he can by making further observations and keeping an eye out for conflicts. But, as the sentences undergoing translation get further and further from mere reports of common observations, the clarity of any possible conflict decreases; the lexicographer comes to depend increasingly on a projection of himself, with his Indo-European *Weltanschauung*, into the sandals of his Kalaba informant. He comes also to turn increasingly to that last refuge of all scientists, the appeal to internal simplicity of his growing system.

The finished lexicon is a case, evidently, of *ex pede Herculem*. But there is a difference. In projecting Hercules from the foot we risk error, but we may derive comfort from the fact that there is something to be wrong about. In the case of the lexicon, pending some definition of synonymy, we have no statement of the problem; we have nothing for the lexicographer to be right or wrong about.

Quite possibly the ultimately fruitful notion of synonymy will be one of degree: not the dyadic relation of a as synonymous with b, but the tetradic relation of a as more synonymous with b than c with d. But to classify the notion as a matter of degree is not to explain it; we shall still want a criterion or at least a definition for our tetradic relation. The big difficulty to be surmounted in devising a definition, whether of a dyadic relation of absolute synonymy or a tetradic relation of comparative synonymy, is the difficulty of making up our minds as to just what we are trying to do when we translate a Kalaba statement which is not a mere report on fairly directly observable features of the surrounding situation.

The other branch of the problem of meaning, namely the problem of defining significant sequence, led us into a contrary-to-fact conditional: a significant sequence is one that *could* be uttered without such and such adverse reactions. I urged that the operational content of this 'could' is incomplete, leaving scope for free supplementary determinations of a grammatical theory in the light of simplicity considerations. But we are well schooled in acquiescing in contrary-to-fact conditionals. In the case of synonymy the tyranny of the developing system, the paucity of explicit objective controls, is more conspicuous.

IV

IDENTITY, OSTENSION,
AND HYPOSTASIS

1

Identity is a popular source of philosophical perplexity. Undergoing change as I do, how can I be said to continue to be myself? Considering that a complete replacement of my material substance takes place every few years, how can I be said to continue to be I for more than such a period at best?

It would be agreeable to be driven, by these or other considerations, to belief in a changeless and therefore immortal soul as the vehicle of my persisting self-identity. But we should be less eager to embrace a parallel solution of Heracleitus's parallel problem regarding a river: "You cannot bathe in the same river twice, for new waters are ever flowing in upon you."

The solution of Heracleitus's problem, though familiar, will afford a convenient approach to some less familiar matters. The truth is that you *can* bathe in the same *river* twice, but not in the same river stage. You can bathe in two river stages which are stages of the same river, and this is what constitutes bathing in the same river twice. A river is a process through time, and the river stages are its momentary parts. Identification of the river bathed in once with the river bathed in again is just what determines our subject matter to be a river process as opposed to a river stage.

Let me speak of any multiplicity of water molecules as a *water*. Now a river stage is at the same time a water stage, but two stages of the same river are not in general stages of the same

65

water. River stages are water stages, but rivers are not waters. You may bathe in the same river twice without bathing in the same water twice, and you may, in these days of fast transportation, bathe in the same water twice while bathing in two different rivers.

We begin, let us imagine, with momentary things and their interrelations. One of these momentary things, called a, is a momentary stage of the river Caÿster, in Lydia, around 400 B.C. Another, called b, is a momentary stage of the Caÿster two days later. A third, c, is a momentary stage, at this same latter date, of the same multiplicity of water molecules which were in the river at the time of a. Half of c is in the lower Caÿster valley, and the other half is to be found at diffuse points in the Aegean Sea. Thus a, b, and c are three objects, variously related. We may say that a and b stand in the relation of river kinship, and that a and c stand in the relation of water kinship.

Now the introduction of rivers as single entities, namely, processes or time-consuming objects, consists substantially in reading identity in place of river kinship. It would be wrong, indeed, to say that a and b are identical; they are merely river-kindred. But if we were to point to a, and then wait the required two days and point to b, and affirm identity of the objects pointed to, we should thereby show that our pointing was intended not as a pointing to two kindred river stages but as a pointing to a single river which included them both. The imputation of identity is essential, here, to fixing the reference of the ostension.

These reflections are reminiscent of Hume's account of our idea of external objects. Hume's theory was that the idea of external objects arises from an error of identification. Various similar impressions separated in time are mistakenly treated as identical; and then, as a means of resolving this contradiction of identifying momentary events which are separated in time, we invent a new nonmomentary object to serve as subject matter of our statement of identity. Hume's charge of erroneous identification here is interesting as a psychological conjecture on origins, but there is no need for us to share that conjecture.

The important point to observe is merely the direct connection between identity and the positing of processes, or time-extended objects. To impute identity rather than river kinship is to talk of the river Caÿster rather than of a and b.

Pointing is of itself ambiguous as to the temporal spread of the indicated object. Even given that the indicated object is to be a process with considerable temporal spread, and hence a summation of momentary objects, still pointing does not tell us *which* summation of momentary objects is intended, beyond the fact that the momentary object at hand is to be in the desired summation. Pointing to a, if construed as referring to a time-extended process and not merely to the momentary object a, could be interpreted either as referring to the river Caÿster of which a and b are stages, or as referring to the water of which a and c are stages, or as referring to any one of an unlimited number of further less natural summations to which a also belongs.

Such ambiguity is commonly resolved by accompanying the pointing with such words as 'this river', thus appealing to a prior concept of a river as one distinctive type of time-consuming process, one distinctive form of summation of momentary objects. Pointing to a and saying 'this river'—or ὅδε ὁ ποταμός, since we are in 400 B.C.—leaves no ambiguity as to the object of reference if the word 'river' itself is already intelligible. 'This river' means 'the riverish summation of momentary objects which contains this momentary object'.

But here we have moved beyond pure ostension and have assumed conceptualization. Now suppose instead that the general term 'river' is not yet understood, so that we cannot specify the Caÿster by pointing and saying 'This river is the Caÿster.' Suppose also that we are deprived of other descriptive devices. What we may do then is point to a and two days later to b and say each time, 'This is the Caÿster.' The word 'this' so used must have referred not to a nor to b, but beyond to something more inclusive, identical in the two cases. Our specification of the Caÿster is not yet unique, however, for we might still mean any of a vast variety of other collections of momentary objects, related in other modes than that of river kinship; all we know is that a and b are among its constituents. By pointing to more and more stages additional to a and b, however, we eliminate more and more alternatives, until our listener, aided by his own tendency to favor the most natural groupings, has grasped the idea of the Caÿster. His learning of this idea is an induction: from our grouping the sample momentary objects a, b, d, g, and others under the head of Caÿster, he projects a correct general hypothesis as to what further momentary objects we would also be content to include.

Actually there is in the case of the Caÿster the question of its extent in space as well as in time. Our sample pointings need to be made not only on a variety of dates, but at various points up and down stream, if our listener is to have a representative basis for his inductive generalization as to the intended spatio-temporal spread of the four-dimensional object Caÿster.

In ostension, spatial spread is not wholly separable from temporal spread, for the successive ostensions which provide samples over the spatial spread are bound to consume time. The inseparability of space and time characteristic of relativity theory is foreshadowed, if only superficially, in this simple situation of ostension.

The concept of identity, then, is seen to perform a central function in the specifying of spatio-temporally broad objects by ostension. Without identity, n acts of ostension merely specify up to n objects, each of indeterminate spatio-temporal spread. But when we affirm identity of object from ostension to ostension, we cause our n ostensions to refer to the same large object, and so afford our listener an inductive ground from which to guess the intended reach of that object. Pure ostension plus identification conveys, with the help of some induction, spatio-temporal spread.

2

Now between what we have thus far observed and the ostensive explanation of *general* terms, such as 'red' or 'river', there is an evident similarity. When I point in a direction where red is visible and say 'This is red', and repeat the performance at various places over a period of time, I provide an inductive basis for gauging the intended spread of the attribute of redness. The difference would seem to be merely that the spread concerned here is a conceptual spread, generality, rather than spatio-temporal spread.

And is this really a difference? Let us try shifting our point of view so far as to think of the word 'red' in full analogy to 'Caÿster'. By pointing and saying 'This is Caÿster' at various times and places, we progressively improve our listener's understanding as to what portions of space-time we intend our word 'Caÿster' to cover; and by pointing and saying 'This is red' at various times and places, we progressively improve our listener's understanding as to what portions of space-time we intend our word 'red' to cover. The regions to which 'red' applies are indeed not continuous with one another as those are to which 'Caÿster' applies, but this surely is an irrelevant detail; 'red' surely is not to be opposed to 'Caÿster', as abstract to concrete, merely because of discontinuity in geometrical shape. The territory of the United States including Alaska is discontinuous, but it is none the less a single concrete object; and so is a bedroom suite, or a scattered deck of cards. Indeed every physical object that is not subatomic is, according to physics, made up of spatially separated parts. So why not view 'red' quite on a par with 'Caÿster', as naming a single concrete object extended in space and time? From this point of view, to say that a certain drop is red is to affirm a simple spatio-temporal relation between two concrete objects; the one object, the drop, is a spatio-temporal part of the other, red, just as a certain waterfall is a spatio-temporal part of Caÿster.

Before proceeding to consider how it is that a general equating of universals to particulars breaks down, I want to go back and examine more closely the ground we have already been over. We have seen how identity and ostension are combined in conceptualizing extended objects, but we have not asked why. What is the survival value of this practice? Identity is more convenient than river kinship or other relations, because the objects related do not have to be kept apart as a multiplicity. As long as what we may propose to say about the river Caÿster does not in itself involve distinctions between momentary stages a, b, etc., we gain formal simplicity of subject matter by representing our subject matter as a single object, Caÿster, instead of a multiplicity of objects a, b, etc., in river kinship. The expedient is an application, in a local or relative way, of Occam's razor: the entities concerned in a particular discourse are reduced from many, a, b, etc., to one, the Caÿster. Note, however, that from an overall or absolute point of view the expedient is quite opposite to Occam's razor, for the multiple entities a, b, etc., have not been dropped from the universe; the Caÿster has simply been added. There are contexts in which we shall still need to speak differentially of a, b, and others rather than speaking indiscriminately of the Caÿster. Still the Caÿster remains a convenient addition to our ontology because of the contexts in which it does effect economy.

Consider, somewhat more generally, a discourse about momentary objects all of which happen still to be river stages, but not entirely river-kindred. If it happens in this particular discourse that whatever is affirmed of any momentary object is affirmed also of every other which is river-kindred to it, so that no distinctions between stages of the same river are relevant, then clearly we can gain simplicity by representing our subject matter as comprising a few rivers rather than the many river stages. Diversities remain among our new objects, the rivers, but no diversities remain beyond the needs of the discourse with which we are occupied.

I have been speaking just now of integration of momentary objects into time-consuming wholes, but it is clear that similar remarks apply to integration of individually indicable localities into spatially extensive wholes. Where what we want to say about certain broad surfaces does not concern distinctions between their parts, we simplify our discourse by making its objects as few and large as we can—taking the various broad surfaces as single objects.

Analogous remarks hold, and very conspicuously, for conceptual integration—the integrating of particulars into a universal. Suppose a discourse about person stages, and suppose that whatever is said about any person stage, in this particular discourse, applies equally to all person stages which make the same amount of money. Our discourse is simplified, then, by shifting its subject matter from person stages to income groups. Distinctions immaterial to the discourse at hand are thus extruded from the subject matter.

In general we might propound this maxim of the *identification of indiscernibles:* Objects indistinguishable from one another within the terms of a given discourse should be construed as identical for that discourse. More accurately: the references to the original objects should be reconstrued for purposes of the discourse as referring to other and fewer objects, in such a way that indistinguishable originals give way each to the same new object.

For a striking example of the application of this maxim, consider the familiar so-called propositional calculus.[1] To begin with, let us follow the lead of some modern literature by thinking of the 'p', 'q', etc. of this calculus as referring to propositional concepts, whatever they may be. But we know that propositional concepts alike in truth value are indistinguishable within the terms of this calculus, interchangeable so far as anything expressible in this calculus is concerned. Then the canon of identification of indiscernibles directs us to reconstrue 'p', 'q', etc., as referring merely to truth values—which, by the way, was Frege's interpretation of this calculus.

For my own part, I prefer to think of 'p', 'q', etc., as schematic letters standing in place of statements but not referring at all. But if they are to be treated as referring, the maxim is in order.

Our maxim of identification of indiscernibles is relative to a discourse, and hence vague in so far as the cleavage between discourses is vague. It applies best when the discourse is neatly closed, like the propositional calculus; but discourse generally

---

[1] See below, pp. 108–113.

departmentalizes itself to some degree, and this degree will tend
to determine where and to what degree it may prove convenient
to invoke the maxim of identification of indiscernibles.

3

Now let us return to our reflections on the nature of universals. Earlier we represented this category by the example
'red', and found this example to admit of treatment as an ordinary spatio-temporally extended particular on a par with the
Caÿster. Red was the largest red thing in the universe—the scattered total thing whose parts are all the red things. Similarly, in
the recent example of income groups, each income group can be
thought of simply as the scattered total spatio-temporal thing
which is made up of the appropriate person stages, various
stages of various persons. An income group is just as concrete
as a river or a person, and, like a person, it is a summation of
person stages. It differs from a person merely in that the person
stages which go together to make up an income group are another assortment than those which go together to make up a person. Income groups are related to persons much as waters are
related to rivers; for it will be recalled that the momentary object a was part in a temporal way both of a river and of a water,
while b was a part of the same river but not of the same water,
and c was a part of the same water but not of the same river. Up
to now, therefore, the distinction between spatio-temporal integration and conceptual integration appears idle; all is spatio-
temporal integration.

Now let me switch to a more artificial example. Suppose our
subject matter consists of the visibly outlined convex regions,
small and large, in this figure. There are 33 such regions. Suppose

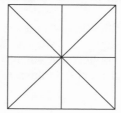

further that we undertake a discourse relatively to which any geometrically similar regions are interchangeable. Then our maxim of identification of indiscernibles directs us for purposes of this discourse to speak not of similarity but of identity; to say not that x and y are similar but that $x = y$, thus reconstruing the objects x and y as no longer regions but shapes. The subject matter then shrinks in multiplicity from 33 to 5: the isosceles right triangle, the square, the two-to-one rectangle, and two forms of trapezoid.

Each of these five is a universal. Now just as we have reconstrued the color red as the total spatio-temporal thing made up of all the red things, so suppose we construe the shape square as the total region made up by pooling all the five square regions. Suppose also we construe the shape isosceles right triangle as the total region made up by pooling all the 16 triangular regions. Similarly suppose we construe the shape two-to-one rectangle as the total region made up by pooling the four two-to-one rectangular regions; and similarly for the two trapezoidal shapes. Clearly this leads to trouble, for our five shapes then all reduce to one, the total region. Pooling all the triangular regions gives simply the total square region; pooling all the square regions gives the same; and similarly for the other three shapes. We should end up, intolerably, by concluding identity among the five shapes.

So the theory of universals as concrete, which happened to work for red, breaks down in general.[2] We can imagine that universals in general, as entities, insinuated themselves into our ontology in the following way. First we formed the habit of introducing spatio-temporally extended concrete things, according to the pattern considered earlier. Red entered with Caÿster and the others as a concrete thing. Finally triangle, square, and other universals were swept in on a faulty analogy with red and its ilk.

Purely as philosophical sport, without supposing there to be any serious psychological or anthropological import in our reflections, let us now go back to Hume's theory of external objects

[2] Cf. Goodman, pp. 46–51.

and carry it a step further. Momentary impressions, according to Hume, are wrongly identified with one another on the basis of resemblance. Then, to resolve the paradox of identity among temporally disparate entities, we invent time-consuming objects as objects of the identity. Spatial spread, beyond what is given momentarily in an impression, may be supposed introduced in similar fashion. The entity red, call it a universal or a widespread particular as you please, may be viewed as entering by the same process (though we are now beyond Hume). Momentary local- ized red impressions are identified one with another, and then a single entity red is appealed to as vehicle of these otherwise un- tenable identities. Similarly for the entity square, and the entity triangle. Square impressions are identified with one another, and then the single entity square is imported as vehicle for the iden- tity; and correspondingly for triangle.

So far, no difference is noted between the introduction of particulars and universals. But in retrospect we have to recog- nize a difference. If square and triangle were related to the origi- nal square and triangular particulars in the way in which con- crete objects are related to their momentary stages and spatial fragments, then square and triangle would turn out to be identi- cal with each other—as lately observed in terms of our artificial little universe of regions.

Therefore we come to recognize two different types of asso- ciation : that of concrete parts in a concrete whole, and that of concrete instances in an abstract universal. We come to recog- nize a divergence between two senses of 'is': 'This is the Caÿster' versus 'This is square'.

4

Interrupting this speculative psychology, let us return to our analysis of ostension of spatio-temporally extended objects, and see how it differs from what may be called the ostension of irreducible universals such as square and triangle. In ostensively explaining the Caÿster we point to a, b, and other stages, and say each time 'This is the Caÿster', identity of indicated object being understood from each occasion to the next. In ostensively explaining 'square', on the other hand, we point to various particulars and say each time 'This is square' *without* imputing identity of indicated object from one occasion to the next. These various latter pointings give our listener the basis for a reasonable induction as to what we might in general be willing to point out as square, just as our various former pointings gave him the basis for a reasonable induction as to what we might willingly point to as the Caÿster. The difference in the two cases is merely that in the one case an identical indicated object is supposed, and in the other case not. In the second case what is supposed to be identical from pointing to pointing is not the indicated object, but, at best, an attribute squareness which is *shared by* the indicated objects.

Actually there is no need, up to this point, to suppose such entities as attributes at all in our ostensive clarification of 'square'. We are clarifying, by our various pointings, our use of the words 'is square'; but neither is an object squareness supposed as object pointed to, nor need it be supposed available as reference of the word 'square'. No more need be demanded, in explication of 'is square' or any other phrase, than that our listener learn when to expect us to apply it to an object and when not; there is no need for the phrase itself to be a name in turn of a separate object of any kind.

These contrasts, then, have emerged between general terms and singular terms. First, the ostensions which introduce a general term differ from those which introduce a singular term in that the former do not impute identity of indicated object between occasions of pointing. Second, the general term does not, or need not, purport to be a name in turn of a separate entity of any sort, whereas the singular term does.

These two observations are not independent of each other. The accessibility of a term to identity contexts was urged by Frege [3] as the standard by which to judge whether that term is being used as a name. Whether or not a term is being used as naming an entity is to be decided, in any given context, by whether or not the term is viewed as subject in that context to the algorithm of identity: the law of putting equals for equals.[3]

It is not to be supposed that this doctrine of Frege's is connected with a repudiation of abstract entities. On the contrary, we remain free to admit names of abstract entities; and, according to Frege's criterion, such admission will consist precisely in admitting abstract terms to identity contexts subject to the regular laws of identity. Frege himself, incidentally, was rather a Platonist in his own philosophy.

It is clearest, I think, to view this step of hypostasis of abstract entities as an additional step which follows after the introduction of the corresponding general terms. First we may suppose the idiom 'This is square', or 'x is square', introduced—perhaps by ostension as previously considered, or perhaps by other channels, such as the usual geometrical definition in terms of prior general terms. Then as a separate step we derive the attribute *squareness*, or, what comes to much the same thing, *the class of squares*. A new fundamental operator 'class of', or '-ness', is appealed to in this step.

I attach much importance to the traditional distinction between general terms and abstract singular terms, 'square' versus 'squareness', because of the ontological point: use of the general term does not of itself commit us to the admission of a corresponding abstract entity into our ontology; on the other hand the use of an abstract singular term, subject to the standard behavior of singular terms such as the law of putting equals for equals, flatly commits us to an abstract entity named by the term.[4]

It is readily conceivable that it was precisely because of failure to observe this distinction that abstract entities gained their hold upon our imaginations in the first place. Ostensive explanation of general terms such as 'square' is, we have seen, much like that of concrete singular terms such as 'Caÿster', and indeed there are cases such as 'red' where no difference need be made at all. Hence the natural tendency not only to introduce general terms along with singular ones, but to treat them on a

[3] See below, pp. 139f.
[4] See also below, pp. 113f.

par as names each of a single entity. This tendency is no doubt encouraged by the fact that it is often convenient for purely syntactical reasons, reasons, for example, of word order or cross-reference, to handle a general term like a proper name.

5

The conceptual scheme in which we grew up is an eclectic heritage, and the forces which conditioned its evolution from the days of Java man onward[5] are a matter of conjecture. Expressions for physical objects must have occupied a focal position from the earliest linguistic periods, because such objects provided relatively fixed points of reference for language as a social development. General terms also must have appeared at an early stage, because similar stimuli tend psychologically to induce similar responses; similar objects tend to be called by the same word. We have seen, indeed, that the ostensive acquisition of a concrete general term proceeds in much the same way as that of a concrete singular term. The adoption of abstract singular terms, carrying with it the positing of abstract entities, is a further step and a philosophically revolutionary one; yet we have seen how this step in turn could have been made without conscious invention.

There is every reason to rejoice that general terms are with us, whatever the cause. Clearly language would be impossible without them, and thought would come to very little. On the admission of abstract entities, however, as named by abstract singular terms, there is room for divergent value judgments. For clarity it is important in any case to recognize in their introduction an additional operator, 'class of' or '-ness'. Perhaps, as just now suggested, it was failure to appreciate the intrusion of such an additional unexplained operator that engendered belief in abstract entities. But this genetic point is independent of the question whether abstract entities, once with us, are not

[5] The unrefined, untutored mind
  Of *Homo javanensis*
  Could only treat of things concrete
  And present to the senses.

a good thing from the point of view of conceptual convenience after all—happy accident though their adoption may have been.

Anyway, once abstract entities are admitted, our conceptual mechanism goes on and generates an unending hierarchy of further abstractions as a matter of course. For, it must be noted to begin with that the ostensive processes which we have been studying are not the only way of introducing terms, singular or general. Most of us will agree that such introduction is fundamental; but once a fund of ostensively acquired terms is at hand there is no difficulty in explaining additional terms discursively, through paraphrase into complexes of the terms already at hand. Now discursive explanation, unlike ostension, is just as available for defining new general terms applicable to abstract entities, for example, 'shape' or 'zoölogical species', as for defining general terms applicable to concrete entities. Applying then the operator '-ness' or 'class of' to such abstract general terms, we get second-level abstract singular terms, purporting to name such entities as the attribute of being a shape or zoölogical species, or the class of all shapes or zoölogical species. The same procedure can be repeated for the next level, and so on, theoretically without end. It is in these higher levels that mathematical entities such as numbers, functions of numbers, etc., find their place, according to the analyses of the foundations of mathematics which have been usual from Frege onward through Whitehead and Russell.

The fundamental-seeming philosophical question, How much of our science is merely contributed by language and how much is a genuine reflection of reality? is perhaps a spurious question which itself arises wholly from a certain particular type of language. Certainly we are in a predicament if we try to answer the question; for to answer the question we must talk about the world as well as about language, and to talk about the world we must already impose upon the world some conceptual scheme peculiar to our own special language.

Yet we must not leap to the fatalistic conclusion that we are stuck with the conceptual scheme that we grew up in. We can change it bit by bit, plank by plank, though meanwhile there is nothing to carry us along but the evolving conceptual scheme itself. The philosopher's task was well compared by Neurath to that of a mariner who must rebuild his ship on the open sea.

We can improve our conceptual scheme, our philosophy, bit by bit while continuing to depend on it for support; but we cannot detach ourselves from it and compare it objectively with an unconceptualized reality. Hence it is meaningless, I suggest, to inquire into the absolute correctness of a conceptual scheme as a mirror of reality. Our standard for appraising basic changes of conceptual scheme must be, not a realistic standard of correspondence to reality, but a pragmatic standard.[6] Concepts are language, and the purpose of concepts and of language is efficacy in communication and in prediction. Such is the ultimate duty of language, science, and philosophy, and it is in relation to that duty that a conceptual scheme has finally to be appraised.

Elegance, conceptual economy, also enters as an objective. But this virtue, engaging though it is, is secondary—sometimes in one way and sometimes in another. Elegance can make the difference between a psychologically manageable conceptual scheme and one that is too unwieldy for our poor minds to cope with effectively. Where this happens, elegance is simply a means to the end of a pragmatically acceptable conceptual scheme. But elegance also enters as an end in itself—and quite properly so as long as it remains secondary in another respect; namely, as long as it is appealed to only in choices where the pragmatic standard prescribes no contrary decision. Where elegance doesn't matter, we may and shall, as poets, pursue elegance for elegance's sake.

[6] On this theme see Duhem, pp. 34, 280, 347; or Lowinger, pp. 41, 121, 145.

V

NEW FOUNDATIONS FOR MATHEMATICAL LOGIC

In Whitehead and Russell's *Principia Mathematica* we have good evidence that all mathematics is translatable into logic. But this calls for the elucidation of three terms: translation, mathematics, and logic. The units of translation are sentences; these comprise statements and also open sentences or matrices, that is, expressions abstracted from statements by supplanting constants by variables. Thus it is not held that every symbol or combination of symbols of mathematics, say '∇' or 'd/dx', can be equated directly to an expression of logic. But it is held that every such expression can be translated in context, that is, that all sentences containing such an expression can be systematically translated into other sentences which lack the expression in question and contain no new expressions beyond those of logic. These other sentences will be translations of the original ones in the sense of agreeing with them in point of truth or falsehood for all values of the variables.

Given such contextual translatability of all mathematical signs, it follows that every sentence consisting solely of logical and mathematical notation is translatable into a sentence consisting solely of logical notation. In particular, thus, all principles of mathematics reduce to principles of logic—or to principles, at least, whose formulation needs no extralogical vocabulary.

Mathematics, in the sense here intended, may be understood as embracing everything which is traditionally classed as pure mathematics. In *Principia* Whitehead and Russell present the constructions of the essential notions of set theory, arithmetic, algebra, and analysis from the notions of logic. Geometry is thereby provided for as well, if we think of geometrical notions as identified with algebraic ones through the correlations of analytical geometry. The theory of abstract algebras is derivable from the logic of relations which is developed in *Principia*.

It must be admitted that the logic which generates all this is a more powerful engine than the one provided by Aristotle. The foundations of *Principia* are obscured by the notion of propositional function,[1] but, if we suppress these functions in favor of the classes and relations which they parallel, we find a three-fold logic of propositions, classes, and relations. The primitive notions in terms of which these calculi are ultimately expressed are not standard notions of traditional logic; still they are of a kind which one would not hesitate to classify as logical.

Subsequent investigations have shown that the array of logical notions required is far more meager than was supposed even in *Principia*. We need only these three: *membership*, expressed by interposing the sign 'ϵ' and enclosing the whole in parentheses; *alternative denial*, expressed by interposing the sign '$|$' and enclosing the whole in parentheses; and *universal quantification*, expressed by prefixing a variable enclosed in parentheses. All logic in the sense of *Principia*, and hence all mathematics as well, can be translated into a language which consists only of an infinity of variables 'x', 'y', 'z', 'x'', etc., and these three modes of notational composition.

The variables are to be regarded as taking as values any objects whatever; and among these objects we are to reckon classes of any objects, hence also classes of any classes.

'$(x \epsilon y)$' states that x is a member of y. Prima facie, this makes sense only where y is a class. However, we may agree on an arbitrary supplementary meaning for the case where y is an

---

[1] See below, p. 122.

individual or nonclass: we may interpret '$(x \in y)$' in this case as stating that x is the individual y.[2]

The form '$(—|{-}{-}{-})$', with any statements written in the blanks, may be read 'Not both — and ---', that is, 'Either not — or not ---', that is, 'If — then not ---'. The first reading is best, being least subject to ambiguities of English usage. The compound statement is false if and only if both constituent statements are true.

The quantifier '(x)', finally, may be read 'for all x', better 'whatever x may be'. Thus '$(x)(x \in y)$' means 'Everything is a member of y'. The total statement '(x)---' is true if and only if the formula '---' to which the quantifier is prefixed is true for all values of the variable 'x'.

Now the *formulas* of this rudimentary language are describable recursively thus: if any variables are put for 'α' and 'β' in '$(\alpha \in \beta)$', the result is a formula; if any formulas are put for 'ϕ' and 'ψ' in '$(\phi \mid \psi)$', the result is a formula; and if a variable is put for 'α' and a formula for 'ϕ' in '$(\alpha)\phi$', the result is a formula. Formulas, so described, are the sentences of the language.

If all mathematics is translatable into the logic of *Principia*, and this logic is to be translatable into the present rudimentary language, then every sentence constructed wholly of mathematical and logical devices must be translatable ultimately into a *formula* in the sense just now defined. I will make the translatability of *Principia* apparent, by showing how a series of cardinal notions of that logic can be constructed from the present primitives. The construction of the mathematical notions, in turn, may then be left to *Principia*.

Definitions, which are the medium of all such construction of derivative notions, are to be viewed as extraneous conventions of notational abbreviation. The new notations which they introduce are to be regarded as foreign to our rudimentary language; and the only justification of our introducing such notations, unofficially as it were, is the assurance of their unique eliminability in favor of primitive notation. The form in which a

[2] This interpretation, along with the subsequent postulate P1, results in the fusion of every individual with its unit class; but this is harmless.

definition is expressed is immaterial, so long as it indicates the manner of elimination. The purpose of definitions, in general, is perhaps brevity of notation; but in the present instance the purpose is to signalize certain derivative notions which play important roles in *Principia* and elsewhere.

In stating the definitions, Greek letters 'α', 'β', 'γ', 'ϕ', 'ψ', 'χ', and 'ω' will be used to refer to expressions. The letters 'ϕ', 'ψ', 'χ', and 'ω' will refer to any formulas, and 'α', 'β', and 'γ' will refer to any variables. When they are imbedded among signs belonging to the logical language itself, the whole is to refer to the expression formed by so imbedding the expressions referred to by those Greek letters. Thus '$(\phi \mid \psi)$' will refer to the formula which is formed by putting the formulas ϕ and ψ, whatever they may be, in the respective blanks of '$(\quad \mid \quad)$'. The expression '$(\phi \mid \psi)$' itself is not a formula, but a noun describing a formula; it is short for the description 'the formula formed by writing a left parenthesis, followed by the formula ϕ, followed by a stroke, followed by the formula ψ, followed by a right parenthesis'. The analogous applies to '$(\alpha \in \beta)$', '$(\alpha)\phi$', '$((\alpha)(\alpha \in \beta) \mid \phi)$', etc. Such use of Greek letters has no place in the language under discussion, but provides a means of discussing that language.

The first definition introduces the customary notation for *denial:*

D1. $\sim\phi$ for $(\phi \mid \phi)$.

This is a convention whereby the prefixture of '$\sim$' to any formula ϕ is to constitute an abbreviation of the formula $(\phi \mid \phi)$. Since in general the alternative denial $(\phi \mid \psi)$ is false if and only if ϕ and ψ are both true, an expression $\sim\phi$ as defined will be false or true according as ϕ is true or false. The sign '$\sim$' may thus be read 'not', or 'it is false that'.

The next definition introduces *conjunction:*

D2. $(\phi . \psi)$ for $\sim(\phi \mid \psi)$.

Since $(\phi \mid \psi)$ is false if and only if ϕ and ψ are true, $(\phi . \psi)$ as defined will be true if and only if ϕ and ψ are true. The dot may thus be read 'and'.

The next definition introduces the so-called *material conditional:*

D3. $(\phi \supset \psi)$ for $(\phi \mid \sim\psi)$.

$(\phi \supset \psi)$, as defined, is false if and only if ϕ is true and ψ false. The connective '$\supset$' may thus be read 'if-then', provided that we understand these words merely in a descriptive or factual sense, and do not infer any necessary connection between the antecedent and the consequent.

The next definition introduces *alternation:*

D4. $(\phi \mathbf{v} \psi)$ for $(\sim\phi \supset \psi)$.

It is readily seen that $(\phi \mathbf{v} \psi)$, as defined, is true if and only if ϕ and ψ are not both false. We may thus read '$\mathbf{v}$' as 'or', provided that this word is understood in the sense which permits joint truth of the alternatives.

The next definition introduces the so-called *material biconditional:*

D5. $(\phi \equiv \psi)$ for $((\phi \mid \psi) \mid (\phi \mathbf{v} \psi))$.

A little study shows that $(\phi \equiv \psi)$, as defined, is true if and only if ϕ and ψ agree in point of truth or falsehood. The sign '$\equiv$' may thus be read 'if and only if', provided that we understand this connection merely in a descriptive sense as in the case of D3.

The devices defined so far are called *truth functions*, because the truth or falsehood of the complex statements which they generate depends only on the truth or falsehood of the constituent statements. The use of alternative denial as a means for defining all truth functions is due to Sheffer.

The next definition introduces *existential quantification:*

D6. $(\exists a)\phi$ for $\sim(a)\sim\phi$.

$(\exists a)\phi$ will thus be true if and only if it is not the case that the formula ϕ is false for all values of the variable a: hence if and only if ϕ is true for some values of a. The sign '$\exists$' may thus be read 'for some'; '$(\exists x)(x \in y)$' means 'For some x, $(x \in y)$', that is, 'y has some members'.

The next definition introduces *inclusion:*

D7. $(\alpha \subset \beta)$ for $(\gamma)((\gamma \in \alpha) \supset (\gamma \in \beta))$.

Thus '$(x \subset y)$' means that x is a subclass of y, or is included in y, in the sense that every member of x is a member of y.

The next introduces *identity:*

D8. $(\alpha = \beta)$ for $(\gamma)((\alpha \in \gamma) \supset (\beta \in \gamma))$.

Thus '$(x = y)$' means that y belongs to every class to which x belongs. The adequacy of this defining condition is clear from the fact that if y belongs to every class to which x belongs, then in particular y belongs to the class whose sole member is x.

Strictly, D7 and D8 violate the requirement of unique eliminability; thus, in eliminating the expression '$(x \subset y)$' or '$(z = w)$', we do not know what letter to choose for the γ of the definition. The choice is indifferent to the meaning, of course, so long as the letter chosen is distinct from the variables otherwise involved; but this indifference must not be smuggled in by the definitions. Let us then suppose some arbitrary alphabetical convention adopted to govern the choice of such a distinct letter in the general case.[3]

The next device to be introduced is *description.* Given a condition '---' satisfied by just one object x, the description '$(\imath x)$---' is meant to denote that object. The operator '$(\imath x)$' may thus be read 'the object x such that '. A description $(\imath\alpha)\phi$ is introduced formally only as part of contexts which are defined as wholes, as follows:

D9. $((\imath\alpha)\phi \in \beta)$ for $(\exists\gamma)((\gamma \in \beta) . (\alpha)((\alpha = \gamma) \equiv \phi))$.

D10. $(\beta \in (\imath\alpha)\phi)$ for $(\exists\gamma)((\beta \in \gamma) . (\alpha)((\alpha = \gamma) \equiv \phi))$.

[3] Thus we may stipulate in general that when a definition calls for variables in the definiens which are suppressed in the definiendum, the one occurring earliest is to be rendered as the letter which stands next alphabetically after all letters of the definiendum; the one occurring next is to be rendered as the ensuing letter of the alphabet; and so on. The alphabet is 'a', 'b', . . . , 'z', 'a'', . . . 'z'', 'a''', ... In particular, then, '$(x \subset y)$' and '$(z = w)$' are abbreviations for '$(z)((z \in x) \supset (z \in y))$' and '$(a')((z \in a') \supset (w \in a'))$'.

Let '---' be a condition on x. Then '$(x)((x = z) \equiv$ ---$)$' means that any object x is identical with z if and only if the condition holds; in other words, that z is the sole object x such that ---. Then '$((\imath x)$--- ϵ $y)$', defined as it is in D9 as '$(\exists z)((z \epsilon y) \cdot (x)((x = z) \equiv$ ---$))$', means that y has a member which is the sole object x such that ---; hence that y has as a member *the* x such that ---. D9 thus gives the intended meaning. Correspondingly D10 is seen to explain '$(y \epsilon (\imath x)$---$)$' as meaning that y is a member of *the* x such that ---. If the condition '---' is not satisfied by one and only one object x, the contexts '$((\imath x)$--- ϵ $y)$' and '$(y \epsilon (\imath x)$---$)$' both become trivially false.

Contexts such as $(\alpha \subset \beta)$ and $(\alpha = \beta)$, defined for variables, now become accessible also to descriptions; thus $((\imath\alpha)\phi \subset \beta)$, $((\imath\alpha)\phi \subset (\imath\beta)\psi)$, $(\beta = (\imath\alpha)\phi)$, etc., are reduced to primitive terms by the definitions D7–8 of inclusion and identity, together with the definitions D9–10, which account for $(\imath\alpha)\phi$ etc. in the contexts upon which D7–8 depend. Such extension of D7–8 and similar definitions to descriptions calls merely for the general convention that definitions adopted for variables are to be retained also for descriptions.

Under this convention, D9 itself applies also when β is taken as a description; we thus get expressions of the form $((\imath\alpha)\phi \epsilon (\imath\beta)\psi)$. But here the requirement of unique eliminability calls for a further convention, to decide whether D9 or D10 is to be applied first in explaining $((\imath\alpha)\phi \epsilon (\imath\beta)\psi)$. We may arbitrarily agree to apply D9 first in such cases. The order happens to be immaterial to the meaning, except in degenerate cases.

Among the contexts provided by our primitive notation, the form of context $(\alpha)\phi$ is peculiar in that the variable α lends it no indeterminacy or variability; on the contrary, the idiom 'for all x' involves the variable as an essential feature, and replacement of the variable by a constant or complex expression yields nonsense. The defined forms of context $(\exists\alpha)\psi$ and $(\imath\alpha)\psi$ share this character, for D6 and D9–10 reduce such occurrences of α to the form of context $(\alpha)\phi$. A variable in such a context is called *bound*; elsewhere, *free*.

Free variables are thus limited, so far as primitive notation is concerned, to contexts of the form $(\alpha \, \epsilon \, \beta)$. The definitions D9–10 provide use of descriptions in just such contexts. Descriptions are thereby made susceptible also to all further forms of context which may be devised for free variables by definition, as in D7–8. Our definitions thus provide for the use of a description in any position which is available to a free variable. This serves our purpose completely, for, as just observed, descriptions or other complex expressions are never wanted in the position of bound variables.

The theory of descriptions which I have presented is Russell's in its essentials, but considerably simpler in detail.[4]

The next notion to be introduced is the operation of *abstraction*, whereby, given a condition '---' upon x, we form the class $\hat{x}$--- whose members are just those objects x which satisfy the condition. The operator '$\hat{x}$' may be read 'the class of all objects x such that'. The class $\hat{x}$--- is definable, by description, as *the* class y to which any object x will belong if and only if ---; symbolically,

D11. $\hat{\alpha}\phi$ for $(\imath\beta)(\alpha)((\alpha \, \epsilon \, \beta) \equiv \phi)$.

By means of abstraction, the notions of the Boolean class algebra are now definable just as in *Principia:* the negate $-x$ is $\hat{y}\sim(y \, \epsilon \, x)$, the sum $(x \cup y)$ is $\hat{z}((z \, \epsilon \, x) \mathbf{\vee} (z \, \epsilon \, y))$, the universal class V is $\hat{x}(x = x)$, the null class Λ is $-$V, and so on. Further the class $\{x\}$ whose sole member is x, and the class $\{x, y\}$ whose sole members are x and y, are definable thus:

D12. $\{a\}$ for $\hat{\beta}(\beta = a)$,

D13. $\{a, \beta\}$ for $\hat{\gamma}((\gamma = a) \mathbf{\vee} (\gamma = \beta))$.

Relations can be introduced simply as classes of ordered couples, if we can contrive to define ordered couples. Clearly any definition will serve this purpose if it makes for the distinctness of couples $(x;y)$ and $(z;w)$ in all cases except where x is z

---

[4] See also above, pp. 5ff, and below, pp. 166f.

and y is w. A definition which is readily seen to fulfill this requirement has been devised by Kuratowski:[5]

D14. $(a;\beta)$ for $\{\{a\}, \{a, \beta\}\}$.

That is, the couple $(x;y)$ is a class which has two classes as members; one of these classes has x as sole member, and the other has x and y as sole members.

Next we can introduce the operation of *relational abstraction*, whereby, given a condition '---' upon x and y, we form the relation $\hat{x}\hat{y}$--- which anything x bears to anything y if and only if x and y satisfy the condition. Since relations are to be taken as classes of ordered couples, the relation $\hat{x}\hat{y}$--- is describable as the class of all those couples $(x;y)$ such that ---; symbolically,

D15. $\hat{a}\hat{\beta}\phi$ for $\hat{\gamma}(\exists a)(\exists \beta)((\gamma = (a;\beta)) . \phi)$.

The idiom 'x bears the relation z to y' needs no special definition, for it becomes simply '$((x;y) \epsilon z)$'.[6]

Enough definitions have here been presented to make the further notions of mathematical logic accessible by means directly of the definitions in *Principia*. Let us now turn to the question of theorems. The procedure in a formal system of mathematical logic is to specify certain formulas which are to stand as initial theorems, and to specify also certain inferential connections whereby a further formula is determined as a theorem given certain properly related formulas (finite in number) as theorems. The initial formulas may either be listed singly, as postulates, or characterized wholesale; but this characterization must turn solely upon directly observable notational features. Also the inferential connections must turn solely upon such features. Derivation of theorems then proceeds by steps of notational comparison of formulas.

The formulas which are wanted as theorems are of course

---

[5] The first definition to this purpose was due to Wiener, but it differs in detail from the present one.

[6] The above treatment of dyadic relations is immediately extensible to relations of any higher degree. For, a triadic relation of x, y, and z can be treated as a dyadic relation of x to the couple $(y;z)$; a tetradic relation of x, y, z, and w can next be treated as a triadic relation of x, y, and the couple $(z;w)$; and so on.

just those which are *valid* under the intended interpretations of the primitive signs—valid in the sense of being either true statements or else open sentences which are true for all values of the free variables. Inasmuch as all logic and mathematics is expressible in this primitive language, the valid formulas embrace in translation all valid sentences of logic and mathematics. Gödel [2] has shown, however, that this totality of principles can never be exactly reproduced by the theorems of a formal system, in the sense of 'formal system' just now described. Adequacy of our systematization must then be measured by some standard short of the totality of valid formulas. A fair standard is afforded by *Principia;* for the basis of *Principia* is presumably adequate to the derivation of all codified mathematical theory, except for a fringe requiring the axiom of infinity and the axiom of choice as additional assumptions.

The system here to be presented is adequate to the adopted standard. It embraces one postulate, namely, the *principle of extensionality:*

P1. $((x \subset y) \supset ((y \subset x) \supset (x = y)))$,

according to which a class is determined by its members. It embraces also three rules specifying whole sets of formulas which are to stand as initial theorems:

R1. $((\phi \mid (\psi \mid \chi)) \mid ((\omega \supset \omega) \mid ((\omega \mid \psi) \supset (\phi \mid \omega))))$ is a theorem.
R2. If ψ is like ϕ except that β occurs in ψ as a free variable wherever α occurs in ϕ as a free variable, then $((\alpha)\phi \supset \psi)$ is a theorem.
R3. If 'x' does not occur in ϕ, $(\exists x)(y)((y \,\epsilon\, x) \equiv \phi)$ is a theorem.

These rules are to be understood as applying to all formulas ϕ, ψ, χ, and ω, and to all variables α and β.

Finally, the system embraces two rules specifying inferential connections:

R4. If ϕ and $(\phi \mid (\psi \mid \chi))$ are theorems, so is χ.
R5. If $(\phi \supset \psi)$ is a theorem, and α is not a free variable of ϕ, then $(\phi \supset (\alpha)\psi)$ is a theorem.

R1 and R4 are an adaptation of the propositional calculus as systematized by Nicod and Łukasiewicz. Together, R1 and R4 provide as theorems all and only those formulas which are valid merely by virtue of their structure in terms of the truth functions.

R2 and R5 contribute the technique for manipulating the quantifier.[7] The rules R1, R2, R4, and R5 provide as theorems all and only those formulas which are valid by virtue of their structure in terms of the truth functions and quantification.

P1 and R3, finally, are concerned specifically with membership. R3 may be called the *principle of abstraction;* it provides that, given any condition '---' upon y, there is a class x (namely, $\hat{y}$---) whose members are just those objects y such that ---. But this principle is readily seen to lead to contradiction. For, R3 gives the theorem:

$$(\exists x)(y)((y \in x) \equiv \sim(y \in y)).$$

Now let us take y in particular as x. This step, immediate for intuitive logic, could be accomplished formally by proper use of R1, R2, R4, and R5. We thus have the self-contradictory theorem:

$$(\exists x)((x \in x) \equiv \sim(x \in x)).$$

This difficulty, known as Russell's paradox, was overcome in *Principia* by Russell's theory of types. Simplified for application to the present system, the theory works as follows. We are to think of all objects as stratified into so-called types, such that the lowest type comprises individuals, the next comprises classes of individuals, the next comprises classes of such classes, and so on. In every context, each variable is to be thought of as admitting values only of a single type. The rule is imposed, finally, that $(\alpha \in \beta)$ is to be a formula only if the values of β are of next higher type than those of α; otherwise $(\alpha \in \beta)$ is reckoned as neither true nor false, but meaningless.[8]

In all contexts the types appropriate to the several variables

---

[7] R5 answers to the first part of Bernays' rule (γ), in Hilbert and Ackermann, ch. 3, §5, and R2 supplants (e) and (α).

[8] In particular, then, β in the context $(\alpha \in \beta)$ cannot take individuals as values. The considerations occasioning the footnote to page 82, above, are thus swept away by the theory of types.

are actually left unspecified; the context remains systematically ambiguous, in the sense that the types of its variables may be construed in any fashion conformable to the requirement that 'ϵ' connect variables only of consecutively ascending types. An expression which would be a formula under our original scheme will hence be rejected as meaningless by the theory of types only if there is no way whatever of so assigning types to the variables as to conform to this requirement on 'ϵ'. Thus a formula in our original sense of the term will survive the theory of types if it is possible to put numerals for the variables in such a way that 'ϵ' comes to occur only in contexts of the form '$n \; \epsilon \; n + 1$'. Formulas passing this test will be called *stratified*. Thus the formulas '$(x \; \epsilon \; y)$' and '$((x \; \epsilon \; z) \mid (y \; \epsilon \; z))$' are stratified, whereas '$(x \; \epsilon \; x)$' and '$((y \; \epsilon \; x) \mid ((z \; \epsilon \; y) \mid (z \; \epsilon \; x)))$' are not. It is to be remembered that definitional abbreviations are extraneous to the formal system, and hence that we must expand an expression into primitive notation before testing for stratification. Thus '$(x \subset x)$' turns out to be stratified, but '$((x \; \epsilon \; y) \cdot (x \subset y))$' not.[9]

Imposition of the theory of types upon our system consists in expurgating the language of all unstratified formulas, hence construing ϕ, ψ, etc., in R1–5 as stratified formulas, and adding the uniform hypothesis that the expression to be inferred as a theorem is likewise stratified. This course eliminates Russell's and related paradoxes, by precluding the disastrous use of unstratified formulas such as '$\sim(y \; \epsilon \; y)$' for ϕ in R3.

But the theory of types has unnatural and inconvenient consequences. Because the theory allows a class to have members only of uniform type, the universal class V gives way to an infinite series of quasi-universal classes, one for each type. The negation $-x$ ceases to comprise all nonmembers of x, and comes to comprise only those nonmembers of x which are next lower

---

[9] If a letter a appears in ϕ both as a bound and as a free variable, or as bound in several quantifiers, we may, in testing ϕ for stratification, treat a as if it were a different letter in each of these rôles. But note that this conveniently liberal interpretation of stratification is not necessary, for the same effect can be gained by using different letters in ϕ in the first place. The latter policy would require revision of the convention in the footnote to page 85 above.

in type than x. Even the null class Λ gives way to an infinite series of null classes. The Boolean class algebra no longer applies to classes in general, but is reproduced rather within each type. The same is true of the calculus of relations. Even arithmetic, when introduced by definitions on the basis of logic, proves to be subject to the same reduplication. Thus the numbers cease to be unique; a new 0 appears for each type, likewise a new 1, and so on, just as in the case of V and Λ. Not only are all these cleavages and reduplications intuitively repugnant, but they call continually for more or less elaborate technical maneuvers by way of restoring severed connections.

I will now suggest a method of avoiding the contradictions without accepting the theory of types or the disagreeable consequences which it entails. Whereas the theory of types avoids the contradictions by excluding unstratified formulas from the language altogether, we might gain the same end by continuing to countenance unstratified formulas but simply limiting R3 explicitly to stratified formulas. Under this method we abandon the hierarchy of types, and think of the variables as unrestricted in range. We regard our logical language as embracing all formulas, in the sense originally defined; and the ϕ, ψ, etc. of our rules may be taken as any formulas in this sense. But the notion of stratified formula, explained in terms merely of putting numerals for variables and divorced of any connotations of type, survives at one point: we replace R3 by the weaker rule:

R3′. If ϕ is stratified and does not contain 'x', $(\exists x)(y)((y \in x) \equiv \phi)$ is a theorem.

In the new system there is just one general Boolean class algebra; the negate $-x$ embraces *everything* not belonging to x; the null class Λ is unique; and so is the universal class V, to which absolutely everything belongs, including V itself.[10] The calculus of relations reappears as a single general calculus treat-

[10] Since everything belongs to V, all subclasses of V can be correlated with members of V, namely, themselves. In view then of Cantor's proof that the subclasses of a class k cannot all be correlated with members of k, one might hope to derive a contradiction. It is not clear, however, that this can be done. Cantor's *reductio ad absurdum* of such a correlation consists in forming the class h of those members of the original class k which

ing of relations without restriction. Likewise the numbers resume their uniqueness, and arithmetic its general applicability as a single calculus. The special technical maneuvers necessitated by the theory of types accordingly become superfluous.

Indeed, since the new system differs from the original inconsistent one only in the replacement of R3 by R3′, the only restriction which distinguishes the new system from the original one is the lack of any general guarantee of the existence of classes such as $\hat{y}(y \in y)$, $\hat{y} \sim (y \in y)$, etc., whose defining formulas are unstratified. In the case of some unstratified formulas, the existence of corresponding classes is actually still demonstrable by devious means; thus R3′ gives

$$(\exists x)(y)((y \in x) \equiv ((z \in y) \mid y \in w))),$$

and from this by the other rules we can accomplish the substitutional inference

(1) $$(\exists x)(y)((y \in x) \equiv ((z \in y) \mid (y \in z))),$$

which affirms the existence of a class $\hat{y}((z \in y) \mid (y \in z))$ whose defining formula is unstratified. But presumably we cannot prove the existence of classes corresponding to certain unstratified formulae, including those from which Russell's paradox or similar contradictions proceed. Within the system, of course, those contradictions can be used for explicitly disproving the existence of the classes concerned, by *reductio ad absurdum*.

The demonstrability of (1) shows that the deductive power of this system outruns that of *Principia*. A more striking instance, however, is the axiom of infinity, with which *Principia* must be supplemented if certain accepted mathematical principles are to be derived. This axiom asserts that there is a class

---

do not belong to the subclasses to which they are correlated, and then observing that the subclass h of k has no correlate. Since in the present instance k is V and the correlate of a subclass is that subclass itself, the class h becomes the class of all those subclasses of V which do not belong to themselves. But R3′ provides no such class h. Indeed, h would be $\hat{y} \sim (y \in y)$, whose existence is disproved by Russell's paradox. For more on this topic see my [4].

with infinitely many members. But in the present system such a class is forthcoming without help of the axiom, namely, the class V, or $\hat{x}(x = x)$. The existence of V is provided by R3'; and so is the existence of infinitely many members of V, namely, Λ, $\{\Lambda\}$, $\{\{\Lambda\}\}$, $\{\{\{\Lambda\}\}\}$, and so on.

Supplementary Remarks

In the foregoing pages the use of parentheses, as a means of indicating the intended groupings within formulas, has been introduced as an integral part of the several primitive and defined notations. Grouping comes in this way to be indicated automatically, without need of supplementary conventions. But this procedure, simple in theory, gives rise in practice to a thicket of parentheses which it is convenient and customary to thin out to a perspicuous minimum. Hereafter, accordingly, parentheses will be omitted except where ambiguity would ensue; also, for ease in reading, the surviving parentheses will be varied with square brackets. But the more mechanical style of the foregoing pages may, for its theoretical simplicity, continue to be thought of as the strict and literal notation.

The primitive notation underlying the foregoing development of logic was threefold, comprising the notations of membership, alternative denial, and universal quantification. Now it is worth noting that this choice of primitives was neither necessary nor minimal. We could have done with just two: the notations of inclusion and abstraction which were defined in D7 and D11. For, taking these two as our starting point, we could regain the old three through this series of definitions, wherein 'ζ' and 'η' are to be understood as referring to any variables and also any terms formed by abstraction.

$$\phi \supset \psi \quad \text{for} \quad \hat{a}\phi \subset \hat{a}\psi,$$

$$(\alpha)\phi \quad \text{for} \quad \hat{a}(\phi \supset \phi) \subset \hat{a}\phi,$$

$$\sim\phi \quad \text{for} \quad (\beta)(\hat{a}\phi \subset \beta),$$

$$\phi \mid \psi \quad \text{for} \quad \phi \supset \sim\psi,$$

$$\phi . \psi \quad \text{for} \quad \sim(\phi \mid \psi),$$

$$\zeta = \eta \quad \text{for} \quad \zeta \subset \eta . \eta \subset \zeta,$$

$$\{\zeta\} \quad \text{for} \quad \hat{a}(a = \zeta),$$

$$\zeta \epsilon \eta \quad \text{for} \quad \{\zeta\} \subset \eta.$$

The first and third of the above definitions involve a special trick. The variable a is not free in ϕ or ψ; this is assured by the convention noted earlier in the comment on D7 and D8. Hence $\hat{a}\phi$ and $\hat{a}\psi$ are "vacuous" abstracts, like '$\hat{x}(7 > 3)$'. Now it can be verified from the old definition D11 of abstraction that a vacuous abstract denotes V or Λ according as the statement in it is true or false. Hence $\phi \supset \psi$ as defined above says in effect that $V \subset V$ (if ϕ and ψ are true) or $\Lambda \subset V$ (if ϕ is false and ψ true) or $V \subset \Lambda$ (if ϕ is true and ψ false) or $\Lambda \subset \Lambda$ (if ϕ and ψ are both false). The definition therefore makes $\phi \supset \psi$ true and false in the appropriate cases. Again the definition of $\sim\phi$ says that the class named by the vacuous abstract $\hat{a}\phi$ is included in every class, that is, that it is Λ; so $\sim\phi$ receives the normal sense of negation. The other six definitions are readily seen to endow the defined notations with the intended senses.

Customarily, in logic, inclusion is thought of as applying only to classes; so a question arises as to the intended interpretation of '$x \subset y$', as a primitive notation of this new system, where x and y are individuals. But the answer is already implicit in D7 of the previous system. If we study D7 in the light of the remarks on '$x \epsilon y$' at the beginning of the essay, we find that '$x \subset y$' amounts to '$x = y$' for individuals.

The basis in inclusion and abstraction is more elegant than the earlier threefold basis, but the threefold basis has certain advantages. One is the ease with which we were able to shift from R3 to R3' and drop the theory of types. For, when abstraction is defined as in D11, we are prepared to find that a term formed from a sentence by abstraction sometimes fails to name a class; and this of course is what happens in the system based on R3'. But when abstraction is primitive, it is less natural to allow a term formed by abstraction to fail to name. The thing is not impossible, however, and in fact a rather compact set of axioms and rules for logic based on inclusion and abstraction without types is at hand.[11]

A second advantage of the threefold basis is that the three primitive notations correspond to three parts of logic which it is convenient to develop successively: truth-function theory, quantification theory, and class theory. Thus, in the logic set forth in the earlier pages of this essay, the principles proper to truth-function theory are provided by R1 and R4; quantification theory is completed by adding R2 and R5; and P1 and R3′ (or R3) belong to class theory. In the system based on inclusion and abstraction, the three parts of logic are bound to be scrambled in a single composite foundation. A reason for liking to develop the three mentioned parts of logic separately lies in their methodological contrasts: the first part has a decision procedure, the second is completable but has no decision procedure, and the third is incompletable.[12] A second reason is that whereas the first two parts can be developed in such a way as not to presuppose classes or any other special sorts of entities, the third part cannot;[13] segregation of the parts therefore has the value of segregating the ontological commitments. A third reason is that whereas the first two parts are settled in essential respects, the third part—class theory—is in a speculative state. For comparison of the numerous alternative class theories now at hand or yet to be devised, it is convenient to be able to take for granted the common ground of truth-function theory and quantification theory and concentrate on variations in the class theory proper. The main alternative systems of class theory, not involving types, can in fact be got by just varying R3′.

One such system, Zermelo's, dates from 1908. Its main feature is the rule of *Aussonderung:*

R3″. If ϕ does not contain 'x', $(\exists x)(y)[y \in x \equiv (y \in z \,.\, \phi)]$ is a theorem.

[11] In the last pages of my [6]. For systematizations involving types see [5].

[12] I explain these points briefly in [2], pp. 82, 190, 245ff. They are due mainly to Church [2] and Gödel.

[13] See next essay.

Given any class z in advance, R3″ guarantees the existence of the class of those members of z satisfying any desired condition ϕ, stratified or not. This rule enables us to argue from the existence of containing classes to the existence of contained classes, but it does not give us any classes to begin with (except Λ, which is got by taking ϕ as false for all values of 'y'). So Zermelo has to supplement R3″ with other postulates of class existence. Accordingly he adds special postulates providing for the existence of

(2) $\{x, y\}$, $\hat{x}(\exists y)(x \in y \,.\, y \in z)$, $\hat{x}(x \subset y)$.

For this theory V cannot exist; for, if z in R3″ were taken as V, R3″ would reduce to R3 and lead thus to Russell's paradox. Also $-z$ can never exist for any $z;$ for if $-z$ existed then so would $\{z, -z\}$ in view of (2), and hence so would $\hat{x}(\exists y)(x \in y \,.\, y \in \{z, -z\})$, which is V. For Zermelo's system no class embraces more than an infinitesimal portion of the universe of the system.

Another system, due to von Neumann,[14] divides the universe into things that can be members and things that cannot. The former I shall call *elements*. Postulates of elementhood are adopted of such kind as to provide, in effect, that what exist at all for Zermelo are elements for von Neumann. Further postulates are adopted for the existence of classes generally, elements and otherwise. The effect of these postulates is to provide for the existence of the class of all *elements* satisfying any condition ϕ whose bound variables are restricted to elements as values.

Over the years since the main portion of the present essay was first published, the system based on P1, R1–2, R3′, and R4–5 has come to be referred to in the literature as NF (for "New foundations"); let us adopt this usage. NF has some evident advantages over Zermelo's system, both in point of what classes exist for it and in point of the directness of its rule of class existence, which obviates laborious constructions. Von Neumann's system has indeed equal or greater advantages in the matter of class existence; whatever laboriousness attaches

---

[14] His system has been brought by Bernays [2] into a form more closely resembling the pattern of the present survey.

to proofs of class existence in Zermelo's system, however, carries over to the proofs of elementhood in von Neumann's system.

Now it turns out that we can multiply our advantages and come out with a yet stronger and more convenient system by modifying NF in somewhat the way in which von Neumann modified Zermelo's system. The resulting system, which is that of my *Mathematical Logic*,[15] I shall call ML. In it R3' of NF is supplanted by two rules, one of class existence and one of elementhood. The rule of class existence provides for the existence of the class of all *elements* satisfying any condition ϕ, stratified or not; symbolically it can be rendered simply as R3'' with '$y \epsilon z$' therein changed to '$(\exists z)(y \epsilon z)$'. The rule of elementhood is such as to provide for the elementhood of just those classes which exist for NF.

The superiority of ML over NF can be well illustrated if we address ourselves briefly to the topic of natural numbers, that is, 0, 1, 2, 3, ... Suppose we have somehow defined 0 and $x + 1$. Then we might, following Frege [1], define a natural number as anything that belongs to every class y such that y contains 0 and contains $x + 1$ whenever it contains x. That is, to say that z is a natural number is to say that

(3) $(y)([0 \epsilon y . (x)(x \epsilon y \supset x + 1 \epsilon y)] \supset z \epsilon y).$

Obviously (3) becomes true when z is taken as any of 0, 1, 2, 3, ... Conversely, it is argued, (3) becomes true only when z is taken as 0 or 1 or 2 or 3 or ... ; and the argument to this effect consists in taking the y of (3) in particular as the class whose members are just 0, 1, 2, 3, ... But is this latter argument sound for NF? In a system such as NF where some presumed classes exist and others do not, we may well wonder whether there *is* a class whose members are all and only 0, 1, 2, 3, ... If there is not, then (3) ceases to be an adequate translation of 'z is a natural number'; (3) becomes true of other values of 'z'

---

[15] Revised edition, which incorporates an important correction due to Wang.

besides 0, 1, 2, 3, ... In ML, on the other hand, where 0, 1, 2, 3, . . . are elements and all classes of elements may be conceived to exist, no such quandary arises.

The quandary which has been set forth just now in intuitive terms recurs, in NF, at the level of formal proof in connection with *mathematical induction*. Mathematical induction is the law which says that any condition ϕ which holds for 0, and holds for $x + 1$ whenever it holds for x, holds for every natural number. The logical proof of this law proceeds simply by defining 'z is a natural number' as (3) and then taking y in (3) as the class of things fulfilling ϕ. But this proof fails in NF for unstratified ϕ, through lack of any assurance of there being a class of exactly the things fulfilling ϕ. In ML, on the other hand, there is no such failure; for, given any stratified or unstratified ϕ, ML provides for the existence of the class of all those elements which fulfill ϕ.

Mathematical induction with respect to an unstratified ϕ can be important. It happens, for example, in the proof that there is no last natural number, that is, that $z \neq z + 1$ for all z satisfying (3). This theorem is forthcoming in ML (†677), and is equivalent to saying (†670) that Λ does not satisfy (3). In NF we can prove each of '$\Lambda \neq 0$', '$\Lambda \neq 1$', '$\Lambda \neq 2$', '$\Lambda \neq 3$', . . . and each of '$0 \neq 1$', '$1 \neq 2$', '$2 \neq 3$', . . . , *ad infinitum;* but no way is known in NF of proving that Λ does not satisfy (3), or of proving that $z \neq z + 1$ for all z satisfying (3).[16]

Thus ML would appear to be essentially stronger than NF. Now increased strength brings increased risk of hidden inconsistency. The danger is a real one. The first fully and rigorously developed theory of classes, Frege's, was shown inconsistent by Russell's paradox.[17] Various more recent theories of classes have, by dint of ever more subtle and laborious proofs, been shown inconsistent likewise; such in particular was the fate of an earlier version of ML itself.[18] It is important, therefore, to seek proofs

---

[16] For more on this topic see my [7], and references therein to Rosser and Wang. [Specker now has proofs; see *Proc. N.A.S.* (1953), pp. 972 ff.]

[17] Cf. Frege [2], vol. 2, appendix.

[18] See Rosser; also Kleene and Rosser.

of consistency—though we must recognize that any proof of consistency is relative, in the sense that we can have no more confidence in it than we have in the consistency of the logical system within which the consistency proof itself is conducted.

It is particularly gratifying, therefore, to note that Wang has shown ML to be consistent if NF is consistent. This means that there is no reason whatever not to avail ourselves of the full luxury of ML as over against NF. At the same time it makes for a continuing interest in NF as a channel for further evidence of the consistency of ML; for NF, being weaker, should lend itself more readily to further proofs of relative consistency than ML. It would be encouraging to find a proof, for example, that NF is consistent if von Neumann's system, or better Zermelo's, is consistent.

Another hint that NF is weaker than ML, and that it should lend itself more readily to proofs of relative consistency, may be seen in the fact that R3'—which is really an infinite bundle of postulates—has been shown by Hailperin to be equivalent to a finite list of postulates. His number is eleven, but the number when finite is not significant, for they could be written in conjunction as one, including P1. This means that NF reduces to just truth-function theory and quantification theory plus a single class-theory postulate. On the other hand, no way has been discovered of reducing ML to truth-function theory and quantification theory and a finite list of class-theory postulates.

It was suggested a few pages back that ML stands to NF somewhat as von Neumann's system stands to Zermelo's. But it should be noted that ML outruns von Neumann's system in the matter of class existence. ML provides for the existence of the class of the elements satisfying any condition ϕ whatever, whereas in von Neumann's system the existence of the class is subject to the condition that the bound variables of ϕ be restricted to elements. This is a significant restriction; for a consequence of it is that von Neumann's system is subject, as Mostowski has shown, to the very difficulty over mathematical induction which was noted above for NF. In a way, therefore, von Neumann's system corresponds in strength rather to NF than to ML. This correspondence is suggested also by the fact that von Neumann's system resembles NF in being derivable from a finite set of postulates over and above the theory of truth functions and quantification. Thus ML stands out as a curiously strong class theory. Wang's proof of the consistency of ML relative to NF is the more welcome for this reason.

VI

LOGIC AND THE REIFICATION
OF UNIVERSALS

1

There are those who feel that our ability to understand general terms, and to see one concrete object as resembling another, would be inexplicable unless there were universals as objects of apprehension. And there are those who fail to detect, in such appeal to a realm of entities over and above the concrete objects in space and time, any explanatory value.

Without settling that issue, it should still be possible to point to certain forms of discourse as *explicitly* presupposing entities of one or another given kind, say universals, and purporting to treat of them; and it should be possible to point to other forms of discourse as not explicitly presupposing those entities. Some criterion to this purpose, some standard of ontological commitment, is needed if we are ever to say meaningfully that a given theory depends on or dispenses with the assumption of such and such objects. Now we saw earlier[1] that such a criterion is to be found not in the singular terms of the given discourse, not in the purported names, but rather in quantification. We shall be occupied in these pages with a closer examination of the point.

The quantifiers '$(\exists x)$' and '(x)' mean 'there is some entity x such that' and 'each entity x is such that'. The letter 'x' here, called a bound variable, is rather like a pronoun; it is used in the quantifier to key the quantifier for subsequent cross-refer-

[1] Pp. 12ff.

ence, and then it is used in the ensuing text to refer back to the appropriate quantifier. The connection between quantification and entities outside language, be they universals or particulars, consists in the fact that the truth or falsity of a quantified statement ordinarily depends in part on what we reckon into the range of entities appealed to by the phrases 'some entity x' and 'each entity x'—the so-called range of values of the variable. That classical mathematics treats of universals, or affirms that there are universals, means simply that classical mathematics requires universals as values of its bound variables. When we say, for example,

$$(\exists x)(x \text{ is prime} . x > 1{,}000{,}000),$$

we are saying that *there is* something which is prime and exceeds a million; and any such entity is a number, hence a universal. In general, *entities of a given sort are assumed by a theory if and only if some of them must be counted among the values of the variables in order that the statements affirmed in the theory be true.*

I am not suggesting a dependence of being upon language. What is under consideration is not the ontological state of affairs, but the ontological commitments of a discourse. What there is does not in general depend on one's use of language, but what one says there is does.

The above criterion of ontological commitment applies in the first instance to discourse and not to men. One way in which a man may fail to share the ontological commitments of his discourse is, obviously, by taking an attitude of frivolity. The parent who tells the Cinderella story is no more committed to admitting a fairy godmother and a pumpkin coach into his own ontology than to admitting the story as true. Another and more serious case in which a man frees himself from ontological commitments of his discourse is this: he shows how some particular use which he makes of quantification, involving a prima facie commitment to certain objects, can be expanded into an idiom innocent of such commitments. (See, for example, §4, below.) In this event the seemingly presupposed objects may justly be said to have been explained away as convenient fictions, manners of speaking.

Contexts of quantification, '$(x)(. . .x. . .)$' and '$(\exists x)(. . .x. . .)$', do not exhaust the ways in which a variable 'x' may turn up in discourse. The variable is also essential to the idiom of singular description 'the object x such that . . .', the idiom of class abstraction 'the class of all objects x such that . . .', and others. However, the quantificational use of variables is exhaustive in the sense that all use of bound variables is *reducible* to this sort of use. Every statement containing a variable can be translated, by known rules, into a statement in which the variable has only the quantificational use.[2] All other uses of bound variables can be explained as abbreviations of contexts in which the variables figure solely as variables of quantification.

It is equally true that any statement containing variables can be translated, by other rules, into a statement in which variables are used solely for class abstraction;[3] and, by still other rules, into a statement in which variables are used solely for functional abstraction (as in Church [1]). Whichever of these roles of variables be taken as fundamental, we can still hold to the criterion of ontological commitment italicized above.

An ingenious method invented by Schönfinkel, and developed by Curry and others, gets rid of variables altogether by recourse to a system of constants, called combinators, which express certain logical functions. The above criterion of ontological commitment is of course inapplicable to discourse constructed by means of combinators. Once we know the systematic method of translating back and forth between statements which use combinators and statements which use variables, however, there is no difficulty in devising an equivalent criterion of ontological commitment for combinatory discourse. The entities presupposed by statements which use combinators turn out, under such reasoning, to be just the entities that must be reckoned as arguments or values of functions in order that the statements in question be true.

[2] See above, pp. 85ff.
[3] See above, pp. 94f.

But it is to the familiar quantificational form of discourse that our criterion of ontological commitment primarily and fundamentally applies. To insist on the correctness of the criterion in this application is, indeed, merely to say that no distinction is being drawn between the 'there are' of 'there are universals', 'there are unicorns', 'there are hippopotami', and the 'there are' of '($\exists x$)', 'there are entities x such that'. To contest the criterion, as applied to the familiar quantificational form of discourse, is simply to say either that the familiar quantificational notation is being re-used in some new sense (in which case we need not concern ourselves) or else that the familiar 'there are' of 'there are universals' et al. is being re-used in some new sense (in which case again we need not concern ourselves).

If what we want is a standard for our own guidance in appraising the ontological commitments of one or another of our theories, and in altering those commitments by revision of our theories, then the criterion at hand well suits our purposes; for the quantificational form is a convenient standard form in which to couch any theory. If we prefer another language form, for example, that of combinators, we can still bring our criterion of ontological commitment to bear in so far as we are content to accept appropriate systematic correlations between idioms of the aberrant language and the familiar language of quantification.

Polemical use of the criterion is a different matter. Thus, consider the man who professes to repudiate universals but still uses without scruple any and all of the discursive apparatus which the most unrestrained of platonists might allow himself. He may, if we train our criterion of ontological commitment upon him, protest that the unwelcome commitments which we impute to him depend on unintended interpretations of his statements. Legalistically his position is unassailable, as long as he is content to deprive us of a translation without which we cannot hope to understand what he is driving at. It is scarcely cause for wonder that we should be at a loss to say what objects a given discourse presupposes that there are, failing all notion of how to translate that discourse into the sort of language to which 'there is' belongs.

Also there are the philosophical champions of ordinary language. Their language is emphatically one to which 'there is' belongs, but they look askance at a criterion of ontological commitment which turns on a real or imagined translation of statements into quantificational form. The trouble this time is that the idiomatic use of 'there is' in ordinary language knows no bounds comparable to those that might reasonably be adhered to in scientific discourse painstakingly formulated in quantificational terms. Now a philological preoccupation with the unphilosophical use of words is exactly what is wanted for many valuable investigations, but it passes over, as irrelevant, one important aspect of philosophical analysis—the creative aspect, which is involved in the progressive refinement of scientific language. In this aspect of philosophical analysis any revision of notational forms and usages which will simplify theory, any which will facilitate computations, any which will eliminate a philosophical perplexity, is freely adopted as long as all statements of science can be translated into the revised idiom without loss of content germane to the scientific enterprise. Ordinary language remains indeed fundamental, not only genetically but also as a medium for the ultimate clarification, by however elaborate paraphrase, of such more artificial usages. But it is not with ordinary language, it is rather with one or another present or proposed refinement of scientific language, that we are concerned when we expound the laws of logical inference or such analyses as Frege's of the integer, Dedekind's of the real number, Weierstrass's of the limit, or Russell's of the singular description.[4] And it is only in this spirit, in reference to one or another real or imagined logical schematization of one or another part or all of science, that we can with full propriety inquire into ontological presuppositions. The philosophical devotees of ordinary language are right in doubting the final adequacy of any criterion of the ontological presuppositions of ordinary language, but they are wrong in supposing that there is no more to be said on the philosophical question of ontological presuppositions.

[4] See below, pp. 165ff.

In a loose way we often can speak of ontological presuppositions at the level of ordinary language, but this makes sense just
in so far as we have in mind some likeliest, most obvious way
of schematizing the discourse in question along quantificational
lines. It is here that the 'there is' of ordinary English lends its ser-
vices as a fallible guide—an all too fallible one if we pursue it
purely as philologists, unmindful of the readiest routes of logical
schematization.

Relative to a really alien language L it may happen, despite
the most sympathetic effort, that we cannot make even the
roughest and remotest sense of ontological commitment. There
may well be no objective way of so correlating L with our familiar type of language as to determine in L any firm analogue of
quantification, or 'there is'. Such a correlation might be out of
the question even for a man who has a native fluency in both
languages and can interpret back and forth in paragraph units at
a business level. In this event, to seek the ontological commitments of L is simply to project a provincial trait of the conceptual scheme of our culture circle beyond its range of significance.
Entity, objectuality, is foreign to the L-speaker's conceptual
scheme.

2

In the logic of quantification, as it is ordinarily set up, principles are propounded in this style:

(1) $[(x)(Fx \supset Gx) . (\exists x)Fx] \supset (\exists x)Gx.$

'Fx' and 'Gx' stand in place of any sentences, for example, 'x is
a whale' and 'x swims'. The letters 'F' and 'G' are sometimes
viewed as variables taking attributes or classes as values, for
example, whalehood and swimmingness, or whalekind and the
class of swimming things. Now what sets attributes apart from
classes is merely that whereas classes are identical when they
have the same members, attributes may be distinct even though
present in all and only the same things. Consequently, if we
apply the maxim of identification of indiscernibles[5] to quantifica-

---

[5] See above, p. 71.

tion theory, we are directed to construe classes rather than attributes as the values of 'F', 'G', etc. The constant expressions which 'F', 'G', etc. stand in place of, then, namely, predicates or general terms such as 'is a whale' and 'swims', come to be regarded as names of classes; for the things in place of whose names variables stand are values of the variables. To Church [6] is due the interesting further suggestion that whereas predicates name classes, they may be viewed as having attributes rather as their meanings.

But the best course is yet another. We can look upon (1) and similar valid forms simply as schemata or diagrams embodying the form of each of various true statements, for example:

(2) $[(x)(x \text{ has mass} \supset x \text{ is extended}) . (\exists x)(x \text{ has mass})]$
$$\supset (\exists x)(x \text{ is extended}).$$

There is no need to view the 'has mass' and 'is extended' of (2) as names of classes or of anything else, and there is no need to view the 'F' and 'G' of (1) as variables taking classes or anything else as values. For let us recall our criterion of ontological commitment: an entity is presupposed by a theory if and only if it is needed among the values of the bound variables in order to make the statements affirmed in the theory true. 'F' and 'G' are not bindable variables, and hence need be regarded as no more than dummy predicates, blanks in a sentence diagram.

In the most elementary part of logic, namely, the logic of truth functions,[6] principles are commonly propounded with 'p', 'q', etc. taking the place of component statements; for example, '$[(p \supset q) . \sim q] \supset \sim p$'. The letters '$p$', '$q$', etc. are sometimes viewed as taking entities of some sort as values; and, since the constant expressions which 'p', 'q', etc. stand in place of are statements, those supposed values must be entities whereof statements are names. These entities have sometimes been called *propositions*. In this usage the word 'proposition' is not a synonym of 'statement' (as it commonly is), but refers rather to hypothetical abstract entities of some sort. Alternatively,

---

[6] See above, p. 84.

notably by Frege [3], statements have been taken to name always just one or the other of two entities, the so-called truth values: the true and the false. Both courses are artificial, but, of the two, Frege's is preferable for its conformity to the maxim of the identification of indiscernibles. Propositions, if one must have them, are better viewed as *meanings* of statements, as Frege pointed out, not as what are named by statements.

But the best course is to revert to the common-sense view, according to which names are one sort of expression and statements another. There is no need to view statements as names, nor to view 'p', 'q', etc. as variables which take entities named by statements as values; for 'p', 'q', etc. are not used as bound variables subject to quantifiers. We can view 'p', 'q', etc. as schematic letters comparable to 'F', 'G', etc.; and we can view '$[(p \supset q) . {\sim}q] \supset {\sim}p$', like (1), not as a sentence but as a schema or diagram such that all actual statements of the depicted form are true. The schematic letters 'p', 'q', etc. stand in schemata to take the place of component statements, just as the schematic letters 'F', 'G', etc. stand in schemata to take the place of predicates; and there is nothing in the logic of truth functions or quantification to cause us to view statements or predicates as names of any entities, or to cause us to view these schematic letters as variables taking any such entities as values. It is only the bound variable that demands values.

Let us interrupt our progress long enough to become quite clear on essential distinctions. Consider the expressions:

$$x + 3 > 7, \qquad (x)(Fx \supset p).$$

The former of these is a sentence. It is not indeed a *closed* sentence, or statement, because of the free 'x'; but it is an open sentence, capable of occurring within a context of quantification to form part of a statement. The other expression, '$(x)(Fx \supset p)$', is not a sentence at all, but a schema, if the attitude is adopted toward 'F' and 'p' which was recommended in the preceding paragraph. The schema '$(x)(Fx \supset p)$' cannot be imbedded within quantification to form part of a statement, for schematic letters are not bindable variables.

The letter 'x' is a bindable variable—one whose values, we may temporarily suppose for purposes of the example '$x + 3 > 7$', are numbers. The variable stands in *place* of *names* of numbers, for example, Arabic numerals; the *values* of the variable are the numbers themselves. Now just as the letter 'x' stands in place of numerals (and other names of numbers), so the letter 'p' stands in place of statements (and sentences generally). If statements, like numerals, were thought of as names of certain entities, and 'p', like 'x', were thought of as a bindable variable, then the *values* of 'p' would be such entities as statements were names of. But if we treat 'p' as a schematic letter, an unbindable dummy statement, then we drop the thought of namehood of statements. It remains true that 'p' stands in place of statements as 'x' stands in place of numerals; but whereas the bindable 'x' has numbers as values, the unbindable 'p' does not have values at all. Letters qualify as genuine variables, demanding a realm of objects as their values, only if it is permissible to bind them so as to produce actual statements about such objects.

'F' is on a par with 'p'. If predicates are thought of as names of certain entities and 'F' is treated as a bindable variable, then the values of 'F' are such entities as predicates are names of. But if we treat 'F' as a schematic letter, an unbindable dummy predicate, then we drop the thought of namehood of predicates, and of values for 'F'. 'F' simply stands in place of predicates; or, to speak in more fundamental terms, 'Fx' stands in place of sentences.

If we did not care eventually to use 'x' explicitly or implicitly in quantifiers, then the schematic status urged for 'p' and 'F' would be equally suited to 'x'. This would mean treating 'x' in '$x + 3 > 7$' and similar contexts as a dummy numeral but dropping the thought of there being numbers for numerals to name. In this event '$x + 3 > 7$' would become, like '$(x)(Fx \supset p)$', a mere schema or dummy statement, sharing the form of genuine statements (such as '$2 + 3 > 7$') but incapable of being quantified into a statement.

Both of the foregoing expressions '$x + 3 > 7$' and '$(x)(Fx \supset p)$' are radically different in status from such expressions as:

(3) $(\exists a)(\phi \mathbf{\,v\,} \psi)$

in the sense of Essay V. (3) occupies, so to speak, a semantical
level next above that of '$x + 3 > 7$' and '$(x)(Fx \supset p)$': it stands as
a name *of* a sentence, or comes to do so as soon as we specify a
particular choice of expressions for the Greek letters to refer to.
A schema such as '$(x)(Fx \supset p)$', on the contrary, is not a name of
a sentence, not a name of anything; it is *itself* a pseudo-sentence,
designed expressly to manifest a form which various sentences
manifest. Schemata are to sentences not as names to their objects, but as slugs to nickels.

The Greek letters are, like 'x', variables, but variables within
a portion of language specially designed for talking *about* language. We lately thought about 'x' as a variable which takes numbers as values, and thus stands in place of names of numbers;
now correspondingly the Greek letters are variables which take
sentences or other expressions as values, and thus stand in place
of *names* (for example, quotations) *of* such expressions. Note
that the Greek letters are genuine bindable variables, accessible
to such verbally phrased quantifiers as 'no matter what statement ϕ may be', 'there is a statement ψ such that'.

Thus 'ϕ' contrasts with 'p' in two basic ways. First, 'ϕ' is a
variable, taking sentences as values; 'p', construed schematically, is not a variable (in the value-taking sense) at all. Second,
'ϕ' is grammatically substantival, occupying the place of names
of sentences; 'p' is grammatically sentential, occupying the place
of sentences.

This latter contrast is dangerously obscured by the usage
(3), which shows the Greek letters 'ϕ' and 'ψ' in sentential rather
than substantival positions. But this usage would be nonsense
except for the special and artificial convention of Essay V (p. 83)
concerning the imbedding of Greek letters among signs of the
logical language. According to that convention, (3) is shorthand
for the unmisleading substantive:

the result of putting the variable a and the sentences ϕ
and ψ in the respective blanks of '$(\exists \quad)(\quad \mathbf{v} \quad)$'.

Here the Greek letters clearly occur in noun positions (referring *to* a variable and to two statements), and the whole is a noun in turn. In some of my writings, for example [1], I have insisted on fitting the misleading usage (3) with a safety device in the form of a modified type of quotation marks, thus:

$$\ulcorner(\exists\alpha)(\phi \vee \psi)\urcorner.$$

These marks rightly suggest that the whole is, like an ordinary quotation, a substantive which refers *to* an expression; also they conspicuously isolate those portions of text in which the combined use of Greek letters and logical signs is to be oddly construed. In most of the literature, however, these quasi-quotation marks are omitted. The usage of most logicians who take care to preserve the semantic distinctions at all is that exemplified by Essay V (though commonly with German or boldface Latin letters instead of Greek).

So much for the usage of Greek letters. It will recur as a practical expedient in §§5–6, but its present relevance is simply its present irrelevance. The distinction which properly concerns us in the present pages, that between sentence and schema, is not a distinction between the use and mention of expressions; its significance lies elsewhere altogether. The significance of preserving a schematic status for '*p*', '*q*', etc. and '*F*', '*G*', etc., rather than treating those letters as bindable variables, is that we are thereby (a) forbidden to subject those letters to quantification, and (b) spared viewing statements and predicates as names of anything.

3

The reader must surely think by now that the recommendation of a schematic status for '*p*', '*q*', etc. and '*F*', '*G*', etc. is prompted purely by a refusal to admit entities such as classes and truth values. But this is not true. There can be good cause, as we shall see presently, for admitting such entities, and for admitting names of them, and for admitting bindable variables which take such entities—classes, anyway—as values. My present objection is only against treating statements and predicates themselves as names of such or any entities, and thus identifying the 'p', 'q', etc. of truth-function theory and the 'F', 'G', etc. of quantification theory with bindable variables. For bindable variables we have 'x', 'y', etc., and, if a distinction is wanted between variables for individuals and variables for classes or truth values, we can add distinctive alphabets; but there are reasons for preserving a schematic status for 'p', 'q', etc. and 'F', 'G', etc.

One reason is that to construe 'Fx' as affirming membership of x in a class can, in many theories of classes, lead to a technical impasse. For there are theories of classes in which not every expressible condition on x determines a class, and theories in which not every object is eligible for membership in classes.[7] In such a theory 'Fx' can represent any condition whatever on any object x, whereas '$x \in y$' cannot.

But the main disadvantage of assimilating schematic letters to bound variables is that it leads to a false accounting of the ontological commitments of most of our discourse. When we say that some dogs are white,

(4) $(\exists x)(x$ is a dog $.\ x$ is white$)$,

we do not commit ourselves to such abstract entities as dogkind or the class of white things.[8] Hence it is misleading to construe the words 'dog' and 'white' as names of such entities. But we do just that if in representing the form of (4) as '$(\exists x)(Fx\ .\ Gx)$' we think of 'F' and 'G' as bindable class variables.

We can of course switch to the explicit form '$(\exists x)(x \in y\ .\ x \in z)$' whenever we really want class variables available for binding. (Also we may use, instead of 'y' and 'z', a distinctive style of variables for classes.) Though we do not recognize the general terms 'dog' and 'white' as names of dogkind and the class of white things, genuine names of those abstract entities are not far to seek, namely, the singular terms 'dogkind' and 'the class of white things'. Singular terms naming entities are

[7] See, for example, pp. 92, 96ff above.
[8] See above, p. 13.

quite properly substituted for variables which admit those entities as values; and accordingly we have:

(5) $(\exists x)(x \in \text{dogkind} . x \in \text{class of white things})$

as an instance of the form '$(\exists x)(x \in y . x \in z)$'. (5) is also, like (4),
an instance of the form '$(\exists x)(Fx . Gx)$'; but (4) is not an instance
of the form '$(\exists x)(x \in y . x \in z)$'.

I grant that (4) and (5) as wholes are equivalent statements.
But they differ in that (4) belongs squarely to the part of language which is neutral on the question of class existence,
whereas (5) is tailored especially to fit that higher part of language in which classes are assumed as values of variables. (5)
itself just happens to be a degenerate specimen of that higher
part of language, in two respects; it actually contains no quantification over classes, and taken as a whole statement it is equivalent to (4).

The assimilation of schematic letters to bound variables,
against which I have been inveighing, must indeed be conceded
some utility if we want to slip from the ontologically innocent
domain of elementary logic into a theory of classes or other abstract entities with a minimum of notice. This could be found
desirable either from an unworthy motive of concealment or
from a worthier motive of speculating on origins. Acting from
the latter motive, I shall in fact exploit the procedure in §§4–5.
But the procedure is useful for this purpose precisely because of
its faults.

The fact that classes *are* universals, or abstract entities, is
sometimes obscured by speaking of classes as mere aggregates
or collections, thus likening a class of stones, say, to a heap of
stones. The heap is indeed a concrete object, as concrete as the
stones that make it up; but the class of stones in the heap cannot
properly be identified with the heap. For, if it could, then by the
same token another class could be identified with the same heap,
namely, the class of molecules of stones in the heap. But actually
these classes have to be kept distinct; for we want to say that
the one has just, say, a hundred members, while the other has
trillions. Classes, therefore, are abstract entities; we may call

them aggregates or collections if we like, but they are universals. That is, if there *are* classes.

There are occasions which call quite directly for discourse about classes.[9] One such occasion arises when we define ancestor in terms of parent, by Frege's method: x is ancestor of y if x belongs to *every class* which contains y and all parents of its own members.[10] There is thus serious motive for quantification over classes; and, to an equal degree, there is a place for singular terms which name classes—such singular terms as 'dogkind' and 'the class of Napoleon's ancestors'.

To withhold from general terms or predicates the status of names of classes is not to deny that there are often (or always, apart from the class-theoretic universes noted two pages back) certain classes connected with predicates otherwise than in the fashion of being named. Occasions arise for speaking of the *extension* of a general term or predicate—the class of all things of which the predicate is true. One such occasion arises when we treat the topic of validity of schemata of pure quantification theory; for a quantificational schema is valid when it comes out true for all values of its free (but bindable) variables under all assignments of classes as extensions of the schematic predicate letters. The general theory of quantificational validity thus appeals to classes, but the individual statements represented by the schemata of quantification theory need not; the statement (4) involves, of itself, no appeal to the abstract extension of a predicate.

Similarly there is occasion in the theory of validity to speak of truth values of statements, for example, in defining truthfunctional validity. But there is no need to treat statements as names of these values, nor as names at all. When we simply affirm a statement we do not thereby appeal to any such entity as a truth value, unless the statement happens to have that special subject matter.

It can indeed prove convenient and elegant in special systems to reconstrue statements as names—for example, of 2 and 1, as

[9] See above, pp. 12ff.
[10] Note the analogy between this definition and (3) of p. 98.

in Church's system [1]. This is perhaps better regarded as a matter of making names of 2 and 1 serve the purpose of statements, for the special system; and I have no quarrel with it. Similarly Frege may be represented as making his singular terms, plus membership, do the work of general terms; and with this again, as a means merely of absorbing lower logic into a particular system of higher logic for the sake of elegance, there is no quarrel. Special systems aside, however, it is obviously desirable to analyze discourse in such a way as not to impute special ontological presuppositions to portions of discourse which are innocent of them.

The bulk of logical reasoning takes place on a level which does not presuppose abstract entities. Such reasoning proceeds mostly by quantification theory, the laws of which can be represented through schemata involving no quantification over class variables. Much of what is commonly formulated in terms of classes, relations, and even number, can be easily reformulated schematically within quantification theory plus perhaps identity theory.[11] Thus I consider it a defect in an all-purpose formulation of the theory of reference if it represents us as referring to abstract entities from the very beginning rather than only where there is a real purpose in such reference. Hence my wish to keep general terms distinct from abstract singular terms.

Even in the theory of validity it happens that the appeal to truth values of statements and extensions of predicates can finally be eliminated. For truth-functional validity can be redefined by the familiar tabular method of computation, and validity in quantification theory can be redefined simply by appeal to the rules of proof (since Gödel [1] has proved them complete). Here is a good example of the elimination of ontological presuppositions, in one particular domain.

In general it is important, I think, to show how the purposes of a certain segment of mathematics can be met with a reduced ontology, just as it is important to show how an erstwhile nonconstructive proof in mathematics can be accomplished by constructive means. The interest in progress of this type is no more

[11] See below, p. 128.

dependent upon an out-and-out intolerance of abstract entities than it is upon an out-and-out intolerance of nonconstructive proof. The important thing is to understand our instrument; to keep tab on the diverse presuppositions of diverse portions of our theory, and reduce them where we can. It is thus that we shall best be prepared to discover, eventually, the over-all dispensability of some assumption that has always rankled as *ad hoc* and unintuitive.

4

It may happen that a theory dealing with nothing but concrete individuals can conveniently be reconstrued as treating of universals, by the method of identifying indiscernibles. Thus, consider a theory of bodies compared in point of length. The values of the bound variables are physical objects, and the only predicate is 'L', where 'Lxy' means 'x is longer than y'. Now where $\sim Lxy$. $\sim Lyx$, anything that can be truly said of x within this theory holds equally for y and vice versa. Hence it is convenient to treat '$\sim Lxy$. $\sim Lyx$' as '$x = y$'. Such identification amounts to reconstruing the values of our variables as universals, namely, lengths, instead of physical objects.

Another example of such identification of indiscernibles is obtainable in the theory of *inscriptions*, a formal syntax in which the values of the bound variables are concrete inscriptions. The important predicate here is 'C', where '$Cxyz$' means that x consists of a part notationally like y followed by a part notationally like z. The condition of interchangeability or indiscernibility in this theory proves to be notational likeness, expressible thus:

$$(z)(w)(Cxzw \equiv Cyzw . Czxw \equiv Czyw . Czwx \equiv Czwy).$$

By treating this condition as '$x = y$', we convert our theory of inscriptions into a theory of notational forms, where the values of the variables are no longer individual inscriptions, but the abstract notational shapes of inscriptions.

This method of abstracting universals is quite reconcilable with nominalism, the philosophy according to which there are really no universals at all. For the universals may be regarded as entering here merely as a manner of speaking—through the metaphorical use of the identity sign for what is really not identity but sameness of length, in the one example, or notational likeness in the other example. In abstracting universals by identification of indiscernibles, we do no more than rephrase the same old system of particulars.

Unfortunately, though, this innocent kind of abstraction is inadequate to abstracting any but mutually exclusive classes. For when a class is abstracted by this method, what holds it together is the indistinguishability of its members by the terms of the theory in question; so any overlapping of two such classes would fuse them irretrievably into a single class.

Another and bolder way of abstracting universals is by admitting into quantifiers, as bound variables, letters which had hitherto been merely schematic letters involving no ontological commitments. Thus if we extend truth-function theory by introducing quantifiers '(p)', '(q)', '$(\exists p)$', etc., we can then no longer dismiss the statement letters as schematic. Instead we must view them as variables taking appropriate entities as values, namely, propositions or, better, truth values, as is evident from the early pages of this essay. We come out with a theory involving universals, or anyway abstract entities.

Actually, though, even the quantifiers '(p)' and '$(\exists p)$' happen to be reconcilable with nominalism if we are working in an extensional system.[12] For, following Tarski [2], we can construe '$(p)(.\,.\,.p.\,.\,.)$' and '$(\exists p)(.\,.\,.p.\,.\,.)$' (where '$.\,.\,.p.\,.\,.$' is any context containing 'p' in the position of a component statement) as the conjunction and alternation of '$.\,.\,.S.\,.\,.$' and '$.\,.\,.\sim S.\,.\,.$', where 'S' is short for some specific statement arbitrarily chosen. If we are working in an extensional system, it can be proved that this artificial way of defining quantification of 'p', 'q', etc. fulfills all the appropriate laws. What seemed to be quantified discourse about propositions or truth values is thereby legitimized, from a nominalist point of view, as a figure of speech.

---

[12] On extensionality see above, p. 30. For a discussion of nonextensional systems see Essay VIII.

What seemed to be discourse in which statements figured as names is explained as a picturesque transcription of discourse in which they do not.

But abstraction by binding schematic letters is not always thus easily reconcilable with nominalism. If we bind the schematic letters of quantification theory, we achieve a reification of universals which no device analogous to Tarski's is adequate to explaining away. These universals are entities whereof predicates may thenceforward be regarded as names. They might, as noted in §2, be taken as attributes or as classes, but better as classes.

In §3 strong reasons were urged for maintaining a notational distinction between schematic predicate letters, such as the 'F' of 'Fx', and bindable variables used in connection with 'ϵ' to take classes as values. The reasons were reasons of logical and philosophical clarity. Now for those very same reasons, seen in reverse, it can be suggestive to rub out the distinction if we are interested in the genetic side. The ontologically crucial step of positing a universe of classes or other abstract entities can be made to seem a small step, rather naturally taken, if represented as a mere matter of letting erstwhile schematic letters creep into quantifiers. Thus it was that 'p' was admitted unchanged into quantifiers a few paragraphs back. Similarly, in the spirit of an imaginative reënactment of the genesis of class theory, let us now consider in detail how class theory proceeds from quantification theory by binding erstwhile schematic predicate letters.

5

First we must get a closer view of quantification theory. Quantificational schemata are built up of schematic components 'p', 'q', 'Fx', 'Gx', 'Gy', 'Fxy', etc. by means of quantifiers '(x)', '(y)', '$(\exists x)$', etc. and the truth-functional operators '$\sim$', '$.$', '$\vee$', '$\supset$', '$\equiv$'.[13] Various systematizations of quantification theory are known which are complete, in the sense that all the valid schemata are theorems. (See above, §3). One such system is

---

[13] See above, pp. 83f.

constituted by the rules R1, R2, R4, and R5, of Essay V, above, if we reconstrue the 'ϕ', 'ψ', 'χ', and 'ω' thereof as referring to quantificational schemata. The definitions D1–6 of that essay must be included.

A conspicuous principle of quantification theory is that for all occurrences of a predicate letter followed by variables we can substitute any one condition on those variables. For 'Fx' we can substitute any schema, for example, '$(y)(Gx \supset Hyx)$', provided that for 'Fz', 'Fw', etc. we make parallel substitutions '$(y)(Gz \supset Hyz)$', '$(y)(Gw \supset Hyw)$', etc.[14] This principle of substitution has not had to be assumed along with R1, R2, R4, and R5, simply because its use can in theory always be circumvented as follows: instead, for example, of substituting '$(y)(Gx \supset Hyx)$' for 'Fx' in a theorem ϕ to get a theorem ψ, we can always get ψ by repeating the proof of ϕ itself with '$(y)(Gx \supset Hyx)$' in place of 'Fx'.

Another conspicuous principle of quantification theory is that of *existential generalization*, which carries us from a theorem ϕ to a theorem $(\exists x)\psi$ where ϕ is like ψ except for containing free occurrences of 'y' in all the positions in which ψ contains free occurrences of 'x'. For example, from '$Fy \equiv Fy$' existential generalization yields '$(\exists x)(Fy \equiv Fx)$'. Now this principle has not had to be assumed along with R1, R2, R4, and R5, simply because whatever can be done by use of it can be done also by a devious series of applications of R1, R2, and R4 (and D1–6).

There is no need to favor R1, R2, R4, and R5 as the basic principles for generating valid quantificational schemata. They happen to be an adequate set of rules, but there are also alternative choices that would be adequate;[15] some such choices include substitution or existential generalization as basic, to the exclusion of one or another of R1, R2, R4, and R5.

Now the maneuver of extending quantification to predicate letters, as a means of expanding quantification theory into class theory, can be represented as a provision merely to allow predi-

---

[14] For a more rigorous formulation of this rule see my [2], §25.

[15] For example, see Hilbert and Ackermann, ch. 3, §5; Quine [1], p. 88; [2], pp. 157–161, 191.

cate letters all privileges of the variables 'x', 'y', etc. Let us see how this provision works. To begin with, the quantificational schema '$(y)(Gy \equiv Gy)$' is obviously valid and hence must be obtainable as a theorem of pure quantification theory. Now our new provision for granting 'F' and 'G' the privileges of ordinary variables allows us to apply existential generalization to '$(y)(Gy \equiv Gy)$' in such fashion as to obtain '$(\exists F)(y)(Fy \equiv Gy)$'. From this in turn, by substitution, we get $(\exists F)(y)(Fy \equiv \phi)$ where ϕ is any desired condition on y.

'F', admitted thus into quantifiers, acquires the status of a variable taking classes as values; and the notation 'Fy' comes to mean that y is a member of the class F. So the above result $(\exists F)$ $(y)(Fy \equiv \phi)$ is recognizable as R3 of Essay V.[16]

Such extension of quantification theory, simply by granting the predicate variables all privileges of 'x', 'y', etc., would seem a very natural way of proclaiming a realm of universals mirroring the predicates or conditions that can be written in the language. Actually, however, it turns out to proclaim a realm of classes *far wider* than the conditions that can be written in the language. This result is perhaps unwelcome, for surely the intuitive idea underlying the positing of a realm of universals is merely that of positing a reality behind linguistic forms. The result is, however, forthcoming; we can obtain it as a corollary of the theorem of Cantor mentioned earlier.[17] Cantor's proof can be carried out within the extension of quantification theory under consideration, and from his theorem it follows that there must be classes, in particular classes of linguistic forms, having no linguistic forms corresponding to them.

But this is nothing to what *can* be shown in the theory under consideration. For we have seen that the theory is adequate to R1–5, including R3; and we saw in Essay V that R1–5 lead to Russell's paradox.

Classical mathematics has roughly the above theory as its

---

[16] See p. 89 above. The hypothesis of R3, namely, that ϕ lack 'x' (or now 'F'), is strictly needed because of restrictions which enter into any rigorous formulation of the rule of substitution whereby ϕ was just now substituted for 'Gy'.

[17] P. 92n.

foundation, subject, however, to one or another arbitrary restriction, of such kind as to restore consistency without disturbing Cantor's result. Various such restrictions were reviewed
earlier.[18] Incidentally, the notation just now developed can be
cut down by dropping the polyadic use of bindable predicate
variables (such as 'F' in 'Fxy'), since relations are constructible
as in Essay V from classes; and the residual forms 'Fx', 'Fy',
'Gx', etc., with bindable 'F', 'G', etc., can be rewritten as '$x \in z$',
'$y \in z$', '$x \in w$', etc. in conformity with what was urged early in
the present essay. We come out with the notation of Essay V.
But in any case universals are irreducibly presupposed. The
universals posited by binding the predicate letters have never
been explained away in terms of any mere convention of notational abbreviation, such as we were able to appeal to in earlier
less sweeping instances of abstraction.

The classes thus posited are, indeed, all the universals that
mathematics needs. Numbers, as Frege showed, are definable as
certain classes of classes. Relations, as noted, are likewise definable as certain classes of classes. And functions, as Peano em-
phasized, are relations. Classes are enough to worry about,
though, if we have philosophical misgivings over countenancing
entities other than concrete objects.

Russell ([2], [3], *Principia*) had a no-class theory. Notations
purporting to refer to classes were so defined, in context, that
all such references would disappear on expansion. This result
was hailed by some, notably Hans Hahn, as freeing mathematics
from platonism, as reconciling mathematics with an exclusively
concrete ontology. But this interpretation is wrong. Russell's
method eliminates classes, but only by appeal to another realm
of equally abstract or universal entities—so-called propositional
functions. The phrase 'propositional function' is used ambigu-
ously in *Principia Mathematica;* sometimes it means an open
sentence and sometimes it means an attribute. Russell's no-class
theory uses propositional functions in this second sense as values
of bound variables; so nothing can be claimed for the theory be-

---

[18] Pp. 90ff, 96ff.

yond a reduction of certain universals to others, classes to attributes. Such reduction comes to seem pretty idle when we reflect that the underlying theory of attributes itself might better have been interpreted as a theory of classes all along, in conformity with the policy of identifying indiscernibles.

6

By treating predicate letters as variables of quantification we precipitated a torrent of universals against which intuition is powerless. We can no longer see what we are doing, nor where the flood is carrying us. Our precautions against contradictions are *ad hoc* devices, justified only in that, or in so far as, they seem to work.

There is, however, a more restrained way of treating predicate letters as variables of quantification; and it does maintain some semblance of control, some sense of where we are going. The idea underlying this more moderate method is that classes are conceptual in nature and created by man. In the beginning there are only concrete objects, and these may be thought of as the values of the bound variables of the unspoiled theory of quantification. Let us call them *objects of order* 0. The theory of quantification itself, supplemented with any constant extralogical predicates we like, constitutes a language for talking about concrete objects of order 0; let us call this language L_0. Now the first step of reification of classes is to be limited to classes such that membership in any one of them is equivalent to some condition expressible in L_0; and correspondingly for relations. Let us call these classes and relations *objects of order* 1. So we begin binding predicate letters with the idea that they are to admit objects of order 1 as values; and, as a reminder of this limitation, we attach the exponent '1' to such variables. The language formed by thus extending L_0 will be called L_1; it has two kinds of bound variables, namely the old individual variables and variables with exponent '1'. We may conveniently regard the orders as cumulative, thus reckoning the objects of order 0 as simultaneously of order 1. This means counting the values of 'x', 'y', etc. among the values of 'F^1', 'G^1', etc. We can explain 'F^1x' arbitrarily as identifying F^1 with x in case F^1 is an individual.[19]

Now the next step is to reify all further classes of such kind that membership in any one of them is equivalent to some condition expressible in L_1; and similarly for relations. Let us call these classes and relations *objects of order* 2. We extend the term to include also the objects of order 1, in conformity with our cumulative principle. So we begin binding 'F^2', 'G^2', etc., with the idea that they are to take as values objects of order 2.

Continuing thus to L_3, L_4, and so on, we introduce bound variables with ever-increasing exponents, concomitantly admitting increasingly wide ranges of classes and relations as values of our variables. The limit L_∞ of this series of cumulative languages—or, what comes to the same thing, the sum of all these languages—is our final logic of classes and relations, under the new procedure.

What we want to do next is specify a theory to much the same effect as L_∞ by direct rules, rather than by summation of an infinite series. For purposes of the general theory certain simplifications can be introduced into the above plan. At the stage L_0 there was mention of some initial assortment of extralogical predicates; but the choice of such predicates is relevant only to applications, and can be left out of account in the formal theory in the same spirit in which we pass over the question of the specific nature of the objects of order 0. Furthermore, as noted in another connection at the end of the preceding section, we can omit the polyadic use of bindable variables; and we can rewrite the residual forms 'F^3x', 'G^2F^3', etc. in the preferred notation '$x^0 \epsilon y^3$', '$y^3 \epsilon z^2$', etc. The notation thus becomes identical with that of Essay V, but with exponents added to all variables. There are no restrictions analogous to those of the theory of types: no requirements of consecutiveness, indeed no restrictions on meaningfulness of combinations. Such a combination as '$y^3 \epsilon z^2$' can be retained as meaningful, and even as true for some values of y^3 and z^2, despite the fact that all members of z^2 are of order 1; for, orders being cumulative, y^3 may well be of order 1.

[19] See above, pp. 81f.

Moreover the rules R1–5 of Essay V can be carried over intact, except that restrictions are needed on R2–3. The restriction on R2 is that *the exponent on β must not exceed that on a*. The reason is evident: if a takes classes of order m as values and β takes classes of order n as values, then all possible values of β will be included among those of a only if $m \geqq n$. The restriction on R3 is that *'y' and 'x' must bear ascending exponents, and ϕ must contain no exponent higher than that on 'x', and none even as high inside of quantifiers*. This restriction reflects the fact that the classes of order $m + 1$ draw their members from order m according to conditions formulable within L_m.

P1 may be retained, but the signs '$\subset$' and '$=$' therein must be redefined now with attention to exponents, as follows: '$x^m \subset y^n$' and '$x^m = y^n$', for each choice of m and n, are abbreviations respectively of:

$$(z^{m-1})(z^{m-1} \,\epsilon\, x^m \supset z^{m-1} \,\epsilon\, y^n), \qquad (z^{m+1})(x^m \,\epsilon\, z^{m+1} \supset y^n \,\epsilon\, z^{m+1}).$$

We then also need, for all choices of exponents, the postulate:

$$x = y \supset (x \,\epsilon\, z \equiv y \,\epsilon\, z).$$

This theory of classes is closely akin to Weyl's, and comparable in power to Russell's so-called ramified theory of types[20] which was proved consistent by Fitch [2]; but it is far simpler in form than either of those systems. It represents, like those systems, a position of conceptualism as opposed to Platonic realism;[21] it treats classes as constructions rather than discoveries. The kind of reasoning at which it boggles is that to which Poincaré (pp. 43–48) objected under the name of *impredicative definition*, namely, specification of a class by appeal to a realm of objects among which that very class is included. The above restriction on R3 is just a precise formulation of the prohibition of so-called impredicative definition.

If classes are viewed as preëxisting, obviously there is no

[20] Without the axiom of reducibility. See below, p. 127.

[21] See above, pp. 14f. The conceptualist position in the foundations of mathematics is sometimes called *intuitionism*, in a broad sense of the term. Under stricter usage 'intuitionism' refers only to Brouwer and Heyting's special brand of conceptualism, which suspends the law of the excluded middle.

objection to picking one out by a trait which presupposes its existence; for the conceptualist, on the other hand, classes exist only in so far as they admit of ordered generation. This way of keynoting the conceptualist position is indeed vague and metaphorical, and in seeming to infuse logical laws with temporal process it is puzzling and misleading. For a strict formulation of the position, however, free of metaphor, we can point to the above system itself.

Let us see how it is that Russell's paradox is now obstructed. The proof of Russell's paradox consisted in taking the ϕ of R3 as '$\sim(y \in y)$', and afterward taking y as x. Now the first of these steps still goes through, despite the restriction on R3. We get:

$$(6) \qquad (\exists x^{n+1})(y^n)[y^n \in x^{n+1} \equiv \sim(y^n \in y^n)]$$

for each n. But the second step, which would lead to the self-contradiction:

$$(7) \qquad (\exists x^{n+1})[x^{n+1} \in x^{n+1} \equiv \sim(x^{n+1} \in x^{n+1})],$$

is obstructed. For, the derivation of (7) from (6) by R1, R2, R4, and R5 would, if carried out explicitly, be found to make use of this case of R2:

$$(y^n)[y^n \in x^{n+1} \equiv \sim(y^n \in y^n)] \supset [x^{n+1} \in x^{n+1} \equiv \sim(x^{n+1} \in x^{n+1})].$$

But this case violates the restriction on R2, in that $n + 1$ exceeds n.

Intuitively the situation is as follows. (6), which holds, assures us of the existence, for any n, of the class of non-self-members of order n. But this class is not itself of order n, and hence the question whether it belongs to itself does not issue in paradox.

The conceptualist theory of classes requires no classes to exist beyond those corresponding to expressible conditions of membership. It was remarked in the preceding section that Cantor's theorem would entail the contrary situation; however, his theorem is not forthcoming here. For Cantor's proof appealed to a class h of those members of a class k which are not members of the subclasses of k to which they are correlated.[22] But this way

[22] See p. 92n above.

of specifying h is impredicative, involving as it does a quantification over the subclasses of k, one of which is h itself.

Thus it is that a theorem of classical or semiclassical mathematics goes by the board of conceptualism. The same fate overtakes Cantor's proof of the existence of infinities beyond the denumerable; this theorem is just a corollary, indeed, of the theorem discussed above. So far, good riddance. But obstacles turn out to confront the proofs also of certain more traditional and distinctly more desirable theorems of mathematics; for example, the proof that every bounded class of real numbers has a least bound.

When Russell propounded his ramified theory of types, these limitations led him to add his "axiom of reducibility." But the adding of this axiom, unjustifiable from a conceptualist point of view, has the effect of reinstating the whole platonistic logic of classes. A serious conceptualist will reject the axiom of reducibility as false.[23]

7

The platonist can stomach anything short of contradiction; and when contradiction does appear, he is content to remove it with an *ad hoc* restriction. The conceptualist is more squeamish; he tolerates elementary arithmetic and a good deal more, but he balks at the theory of higher infinities and at parts of the higher theory of real numbers. In a fundamental respect, however, the conceptualist and the platonist are alike: they both assume universals, classes, irreducibly as values of their bound variables. The platonistic class theory of §5 and the conceptualistic class theory of §6 differ only thus: in the platonistic theory the universe of classes is limited grudgingly and minimally by restrictions whose sole purpose is the avoidance of paradox, whereas in the conceptualistic theory the universe of classes is limited cheerfully and drastically in terms of a metaphor of progressive creation. It would be a mistake to suppose that this metaphor really accounts for the classes, or explains them away; for there is no

---

[23] See my [3].

indication of how the conceptualist's quantification over classes can be paraphrased into any more basic and ontologically more innocent notation. The conceptualist has indeed some justification for feeling that his ground is solider than the platonist's, but his justification is limited to these two points: the universe of classes which he assumes is meagerer than the platonist's, and the principle by which he limits it rests on a metaphor that has some intuitive worth.

The heroic or quixotic position is that of the nominalist, who foreswears quantification over universals, for example, classes, altogether. He remains free to accept the logic of truth functions and quantification and identity, and also any fixed predicates he likes which apply to particulars, or nonuniversals (however these be construed). He can even accept the so-called algebras of classes and relations, in the narrowest sense, and the most rudimentary phases of arithmetic; for these theories can be reconstrued as mere notational variants of the logic of quantification and identity.[24] He can accept laws which contain variables for classes and relations and numbers, as long as the laws are asserted as holding for all values of those variables; for he can treat such laws as schemata, like the laws of truth functions and quantification. But bound variables for classes or relations or numbers, if they occur in existential quantifiers or in universal quantifiers within subordinate clauses, must be renounced by the nominalist in all contexts in which he cannot explain them away by paraphrase. He must renounce them when he needs them.

The nominalist could of course gain full freedom to quantify over numbers if he identified them, by some arbitrary correlation, with the several particulars of his recognized universe—say with the concrete individuals of the physical world. But this expedient has the shortcoming that it cannot guarantee the infinite multiplicity of numbers which classical arithmetic demands. The nominalist has repudiated the infinite universe of universals as a dream world; he is not going to impute infinitude to his universe of particulars unless it happens to be infinite as a

[24] See my [2], pp. 230ff, 239.

matter of objective fact—attested to, say, by the physicist. From a mathematical point of view, indeed, the important opposition of doctrines here is precisely the opposition between unwillingness and willingness to posit, out of hand, an infinite universe. This is a clearer division than that between nominalists and others as ordinarily conceived, for the latter division depends on a none too clear distinction between what qualifies as particular and what counts as universal. In the opposition between conceptualists and platonists, in turn, we have an opposition between those who admit just one degree of infinity and those who admit a Cantorian hierarchy of infinities.

The nominalist, or he who preserves an agnosticism about the infinitude of entities, can still accommodate in a certain indirect way the mathematics of the infinitist—the conceptualist or platonist. Though he cannot believe such mathematics, he *can* formulate the rules of its prosecution.[25] But he would like to show also that whatever service classical mathematics performs for science can in theory be performed equally, if less simply, by really nominalistic methods—unaided by a meaningless mathematics whose mere syntax is nominalistically described. And here he has his work cut out for him. Here he finds the strongest temptation to fall into the more easygoing ways of the conceptualist, who, accepting a conveniently large slice of classical mathematics, needs only to show the dispensability of the theory of higher infinites and portions of real number theory.

Tactically, conceptualism is no doubt the strongest position of the three; for the tired nominalist can lapse into conceptualism and still allay his puritanic conscience with the reflection that he has not quite taken to eating lotus with the platonists.

[25] See above, p. 15.

VII

NOTES ON THE THEORY OF REFERENCE

1

When the cleavage between meaning and reference is properly heeded,[1] the problems of what is loosely called semantics become separated into two provinces so fundamentally distinct as not to deserve a joint appellation at all. They may be called the *theory of meaning* and the *theory of reference*. 'Semantics' would be a good name for the theory of meaning, were it not for the fact that some of the best work in so-called semantics, notably Tarski's, belongs to the theory of reference. The main concepts in the theory of meaning, apart from meaning itself, are *synonymy* (or sameness of meaning), *significance* (or possession of meaning), and *analyticity* (or truth by virtue of meaning). Another is *entailment*, or analyticity of the conditional. The main concepts in the theory of reference are *naming*, *truth*, *denotation* (or truth-of), and *extension*. Another is the notion of *values* of variables.

Boundaries between fields are not barriers. Given any two fields, it is conceivable that a concept might be compounded of concepts from both fields. But if this were to happen in the case of the theory of meaning and the theory of reference, we should probably reckon the hybrid concept to the theory of meaning—simply because the theory of meaning is in a worse state than the theory of reference, and is consequently the more serious of the two presuppositions.

As applied to discourse in an explicitly quantificational form of language, the notion of ontological commitment belongs to the

[1] See above, pp. 9, 21.

130

theory of reference. For to say that a given existential quantification presupposes objects of a given kind is to say simply that the open sentence which follows the quantifier is true of some objects of that kind and none not of that kind. In so far as we undertake to speak of ontological commitment on the part of discourse not in an explicitly quantificational form of language, on the other hand, and to rest our case on a supposed synonymy between the given statements and their translations in a quantificational language, we are of course involved in the theory of meaning.

Given a theory, one philosophically interesting aspect of it into which we can inquire is its ontology. But we can also inquire into its *ideology* (to give a good sense to a bad word): what ideas can be expressed in it? The ontology of a theory stands in no simple correspondence to its ideology. Thus, consider the usual theory of real numbers. Its ontology exhausts the real numbers, but its ideology—the range of severally expressible ideas—embraces individual ideas of only certain of the real numbers. For it is known that no notation is adequate to the separate specification of each real number.[2] On the other hand, the ideology also embraces many such ideas as sum, root, rationality, algebraicity, and the like, which need not have any ontological correlates in the range of the variables of quantification of the theory.

Two theories can have the same ontology and different ideologies. Two theories of real numbers, for example, may agree ontologically in that each calls for all and only the real numbers as values of its variables, but they may still differ ideologically in that one theory is expressed in a language into which the sentence:

(1)   the real number x is a whole number

can be translated, while the other theory is not. Note the importance of this particular example; Tarski [1] has proved the completeness of a certain elementary theory T of real numbers, and we know from Gödel's proof [2] of the incompletability of

[2] See, for example, my [1], p. 273f.

the theory of whole numbers that Tarski's achievement would have been impossible if (1) were translatable into the notation of T.

It is instructive to observe that the ontology of a theory may embrace objects of some kind K even where kind K is not definable in the terms of the theory. For example, the ontology of T can be shown to embrace the whole real numbers despite the fact that (1) is not translatable into the notation of T.

I have described the ideology of a theory vaguely as asking what ideas are expressible in the language of the theory. Ideology thus seems to involve us in the idea of an idea. But this formulation may well be dropped, and with it the term 'ideology'. For such substantial work as would fall under ideology consists precisely of the theory of *definability;* and this theory, far from depending on the idea idea, stands clear of the theory of meaning altogether and falls squarely within the theory of reference. The word 'definition' has indeed commonly connoted synonymy,[3] which belongs to the theory of meaning; the mathematical literature on definability,[4] however, has to do with definability only in the following more innocuous sense. A general term t is said to be *definable* in any portion of language which includes a sentence S such that S has the variable 'x' in it and is fulfilled by all and only those values of 'x' of which t is true. Definability so construed rests only on sameness of reference—sameness of extension on the part of t and S. Definability of expressions of other categories than that of general terms may be explained in fairly parallel fashion. A typical theorem of the theory of definability in this sense, and hence of the theory of reference, is the above observation that 'whole' is not definable in T.

2

In Essays II and III we dwelt on the sorry state of the theory of meaning. The theory of reference, actually, has also had its troubles, for it is the scene of the so-called semantic paradoxes.

[3] See above, pp. 24ff.
[4] Tarski [3]; Robinson; Myhill; Church and Quine. See also p. 80 above.

The best known of those paradoxes is the Epimenides, anciently rendered thus: Epimenides the Cretan says that Cretans always lie; hence his statement must, if true, be a lie. Here obviously we are involved in no real paradox, but only in the conclusion that Epimenides here lies and some Cretans sometimes do not. The situation can be developed into a paradox, however, by adopting three historical premisses: not only (a) that Epimenides was a Cretan and (b) that Epimenides said that Cretans never speak the truth, but also (c) that all *other* statements by Cretans were indeed false. Then Epimenides' statement becomes false if true, and true if false—an impossible situation.

It is instructive to contrast this paradox with the riddle of the barber. A man of Alcalá is said to have shaved all and only those men of Alcalá who did not shave themselves; and we find that he shaved himself if and only if he did not.[5] This is no real paradox, but only a *reductio ad absurdum* proof that there was no such man in Alcalá. On the other hand the Epimenides, as last refined, cannot be thus dismissed. For whereas it is evident that a self-contradictory condition was imposed on the barber, we cannot so unconcernedly acknowledge incompatibility of the three palpably independent conditions (a)–(c).

A variant of the Epimenides paradox, likewise ancient, is the *pseudomenon* of the Megarian school: 'I am lying'. A still simpler version may be put thus:

(2)   (2) is false.

Clearly (2), which reads as above, is false if true and true if false.

In an effort to escape the self-contradictory predicament of having to regard (2) as both true and false, one might protest that (2) is simply meaningless, on the ground that an attempt to expand the reference '(2)' in (2) into a specific quotation of an actual statement leads into an infinite regress. But this protest can be silenced by resorting to a more complex version, as follows:

---

[5] A version of this was attributed by Russell ([4], pp. 354f) to an unnamed acquaintance.

(3)   'does not produce a true statement when appended
         to its own quotation' produces a true statement
         when appended to its own quotation.

The above statement is readily seen to say that its own denial is true.

Another so-called semantical paradox is Grelling's, which consists in asking whether the general term 'not true of itself' is true of itself; clearly it will be true of itself if and only if it is not. A third is Berry's, concerning the least number not specifiable in less than nineteen syllables. That number has just now been specified in eighteen syllables.[6]

These paradoxes seem to show that the most characteristic terms of the theory of reference, namely, 'true', 'true of', and 'naming' (or 'specifying'), must be banned from language as meaningless, on pain of contradiction. But this conclusion is hard to accept, for the three familiar terms in question seem to possess a peculiar clarity in view of these three paradigms:

(4)   '——' *is true* if and only if ——,
(5)   '——' *is true of* every —— thing and nothing else.
(6)   '——' *names* —— and nothing else.

(4) holds when any one statement is written in the two blanks; (5) holds when any one general term (in adjective form, or, omitting 'thing', in substantive form) is written in the two blanks; and (6) holds whenever any one name (which really names, that is, whose object exists) is written in the two blanks.

Strictly, the notions of the theory of reference, and likewise those of the theory of meaning (if they are countenanced at all), are relative always to a language; the language figures, albeit tacitly, as a parameter. Thus it will be recalled that the problem of construing 'analytic' was recognized as the problem of construing 'analytic in L' for variable 'L'.[7] Similarly, a statement, thought of as a string of letters or sounds, is never simply true, but true in language L for appropriate L. This is not a philo-

---

[6] See Whitehead and Russell, vol. 1, p. 61.
[7] See above, pp. 33ff.

sophical doctrine of the relativity of all fact to language; the point is much more superficial. The point is merely that a given string of letters or sounds could constitute at once a statement say of English and a statement (different in meaning, to borrow a phrase) of Frisian, and it might happen in its English meaning to be true and in its Frisian meaning to be false.[8] Properly, therefore, (4)–(6) should appear rather thus:

(7)   '——' is true-in-L if and only if ——,
(8)   '——' is true-in-L of every —— thing and nothing else.
(9)   '——' names-in-L —— and nothing else.

But now it becomes necessary that L and the language in which (7)–(9) themselves are couched (namely, English) be the same, or at least that they overlap to the extent of any notations to which (in the role of '——') we propose to apply (7)–(9). Otherwise we might even get falsehoods as instances of (7)–(9), in the rare event of a coincidence such as was imagined between Frisian and English; but usually we would get mere nonsense, of the type:

(10)   'Der Schnee ist weiss' is true-in-German if and only
         if der Schnee ist weiss.

The quotation at the beginning of (10) is indeed a good English word, constituting a name of a German statement; but the rest of (10) is a meaningless jumble of languages.

If, however, we were to pool German and English to form a composite language, German-English, then (10) could be said to be true in German-English. In general, if language L (for example, German) is contained in language L' (for example, German-English), so that L' is simply L or else L plus some supplementary vocabulary or grammatical constructions, and if the portions, at least, of English usage which figure in (7) above (apart from the blanks) are part of L', then the result of putting any one statement of L for the blanks in (7) is true in L'. Correspondingly for (8); if L is contained in L', and the constant

---

[8] The need to allow in theoretical semantics for such interlinguistic coincidences has been noted in another connection by Church [5].

matter in (8) is part of L', then the result of putting any one general term of L for the blanks in (8) is true in L'. Correspondingly for (9).

Now it turns out that the semantical paradoxes noted earlier do not arise if we take these two precautions: qualify (4)–(6) in the fashion (7)–(9), and banish such terms as 'true-in-L', 'true-in-L of', and 'names-in-L' from the language L itself. These terms, appropriate to the theory of reference *of* L, may continue to exist in a more inclusive language L' containing L; and the paradigms (7)–(9) may then continue to hold in L', without paradox, as long as the statements or terms which fill the blanks belong not merely to L' but specifically to L.

3

It must be noted that the paradigms (4)–(6) were not strictly definitions of the verbs 'is true', 'is true of', and 'names', nor are (7)–(9) definitions of the verbs 'is true-in-L', 'is true-in-L of', and 'names-in-L'. For the paradigms enable us to eliminate those verbs only from positions preceded by quotations; not from positions preceded, for example, by pronouns, or variables of quantification. Nevertheless, the paradigms resemble definitions in this fundamental respect: they leave no ambiguity as to the extensions, the ranges of applicability, of the verbs in question. In the case of (7) this is seen as follows. Supposing two different interpretations of 'true-in-L' compatible with (7), let us distinguish them by writing 'true$_1$-in-L' and 'true$_2$-in-L', and let (7)$_1$ and (7)$_2$ be (7) with these respective subscripts inserted. From (7)$_1$ and (7)$_2$ it follows logically that

'——' is true$_1$-in-L if and only if '——' is true$_2$-in-L,

no matter what statement of L we write for '——'. Thus truth$_1$-in-L and truth$_2$-in-L coincide. Similar reasoning works for (8) and (9).

Tarski, to whom the reflections on truth in the foregoing pages are largely due ([4], [6]), goes on to show further that 'true-in-L' is in fact genuinely definable in L' if certain general circumstances obtain. Let us suppose that L is a language of the general form described on page 30 above, and that the whole vocabulary of predicates of L is fixed in a finished list. Suppose further that L' contains L and, in addition, some specifically linguistic terminology adequate to naming each individual symbol of L and to expressing concatenation of symbols. Suppose finally that L' possesses a normal complement of logical notation, including that of the theory of classes. Now Tarski shows how to formulate within the notation of L' a sentence '$---x---$' which fulfills:

$$---x--- \text{ if and only if} \underline{\hspace{2em}}$$

whenever a statement of L is put for '$\underline{\hspace{2em}}$' and a name of that statement is put for 'x'. In short, he shows that 'true-in-L', in a sense conforming to (7), is definable in L', in a sense of 'definable' conforming to the early pages of the present essay.[9] His actual construction will be passed over here.

In certain formalized notations capable of treating their own grammar or capable of treating some subject matter in which a model of that grammar can be constructed, Tarski's method enables us to derive a form of the Epimenides paradox tantamount to (3). Gödel's theorem [2] of the incompletability of number theory, indeed, can be got by a *reductio ad absurdum* along these lines; such is my method in [1], ch. 7. Generally, if L is not to be involved in the Epimenides, 'truth-in-L' must be definable only in an L' which includes notation for a stronger logical theory (a stronger theory of classes, for example) than that available in L.[10]

Tarski's construction of truth is easily extended to other concepts of the theory of reference. It is a striking fact that these notions, despite the paradoxes which we associate with them, are so very much less foggy and mysterious than the notions

[9] It is sometimes overlooked that there is no need to claim, and that Tarski has not claimed, that the statements of the form (7) (or (8) or (9)) are analytic. This point has been repeatedly set right; cf. Lewy, White [1], Thomson.

[10] See Tarski [4], [5], [6]; also Quine [8]. But if L is especially weak in certain ways, this requirement lapses; witness Myhill's system, which lacks negation.

belonging to the theory of meaning. We have general paradigms (7)–(9) which, though they are not definitions, yet serve to endow 'true-in-L' and 'true-in-L of' and 'names-in-L' with every bit as much clarity, in any particular application, as is enjoyed by the particular expressions of L to which we apply them. Attribution of truth in particular to 'Snow is white', for example, is every bit as clear to us as attribution of whiteness to snow. In Tarski's technical construction, moreover, we have an explicit general routine for defining truth-in-L for individual languages L which conform to a certain standard pattern and are well specified in point of vocabulary. We have indeed no similar single definition of 'true-in-L' for variable 'L'; but what we do have suffices to endow 'true-in-L', even for variable 'L', with a high enough degree of intelligibility so that we are not likely to be averse to using the idiom. No term, of course, is definable except in other terms; and the urgency of the demand for definition is proportional to the obscurity of the term.

See how unfavorably the notion of analyticity-in-L, characteristic of the theory of meaning, compares with that of truth-in-L. For the former we have no clue comparable in value to (7). Nor have we any systematic routine for constructing definitions of 'analytic-in-L', even for the various individual choices of L; definition of 'analytic-in-L' for each L has seemed rather to be a project unto itself.[11] The most evident principle of unification, linking analyticity-in-L for one choice of L with analyticity-in-L for another choice of L, is the joint use of the syllables 'analytic'.

[11] See above, pp. 32–36.

VIII

REFERENCE AND MODALITY

1

One of the fundamental principles governing identity is that of *substitutivity*—or, as it might well be called, that of *indiscernibility of identicals*. It provides that, *given a true statement of identity, one of its two terms may be substituted for the other in any true statement and the result will be true*. It is easy to find cases contrary to this principle. For example, the statements:

(1)   Giorgione = Barbarelli,

(2)   Giorgione was so-called because of his size

are true; however, replacement of the name 'Giorgione' by the name 'Barbarelli' turns (2) into the falsehood:

        Barbarelli was so-called because of his size.

Furthermore, the statements:

(3)   Cicero = Tully,

(4)   'Cicero' contains six letters

are true, but replacement of the first name by the second turns (4) false. Yet the basis of the principle of substitutivity appears quite solid; whatever can be said about the person Cicero (or Giorgione) should be equally true of the person Tully (or Barbarelli), this being the same person.

In the case of (4), this paradox resolves itself immediately. The fact is that (4) is not a statement about the person Cicero, but simply about the word 'Cicero'. The principle of substitutivity should not be extended to contexts in which the name

139

to be supplanted occurs without referring simply to the object. Failure of substitutivity reveals merely that the occurrence to be supplanted is not *purely referential*,[1] that is, that the statement depends not only on the object but on the form of the name. For it is clear that whatever can be affirmed about the object remains true when we refer to the object by any other name.

An expression which consists of another expression between single quotes constitutes a name of that other expression; and it is clear that the occurrence of that other expression or a part of it, within the context of quotes, is not in general referential. In particular, the occurrence of the personal name within the context of quotes in (4) is not referential, not subject to the substitutivity principle. The personal name occurs there merely as a fragment of a longer name which contains, beside this fragment, the two quotation marks. To make a substitution upon a personal name, within such a context, would be no more justifiable than to make a substitution upon the term 'cat' within the context 'cattle'.

The example (2) is a little more subtle, for it is a statement about a man and not merely about his name. It was the man, not his name, that was called so and so because of his size. Nevertheless, the failure of substitutivity shows that the occurrence of the personal name in (2) is not *purely* referential. It is easy in fact to translate (2) into another statement which contains two occurrences of the name, one purely referential and the other not:

(5)   Giorgione was called 'Giorgione' because of his size.

The first occurrence is purely referential. Substitution on the basis of (1) converts (5) into another statement equally true:

    Barbarelli was called 'Giorgione' because of his size.

The second occurrence of the personal name is no more referential than any other occurrence within a context of quotes.

---

[1] Frege [3] spoke of *direct* (*gerade*) and *oblique* (*ungerade*) occurrences, and used substitutivity of identity as a criterion just as here.

It would not be quite accurate to conclude that an occurrence of a name within single quotes is *never* referential. Consider the statements:

(6)   'Giorgione played chess' is true,

(7)   'Giorgione' named a chess player,

each of which is true or false according as the quotationless statement:

(8)   Giorgione played chess

is true or false. Our criterion of referential occurrence makes the occurrence of the name 'Giorgione' in (8) referential, and must make the occurrences of 'Giorgione' in (6) and (7) referential by the same token, despite the presence of single quotes in (6) and (7). The point about quotation is not that it must destroy referential occurrence, but that it can (and ordinarily does) destroy referential occurrence. The examples (6) and (7) are exceptional in that the special predicates 'is true' and 'named' have the effect of undoing the single quotes—as is evident on comparison of (6) and (7) with (8).

To get an example of another common type of statement in which names do not occur referentially, consider any person who is called Philip and satisfies the condition:

(9)   Philip is unaware that Tully denounced Catiline,

or perhaps the condition:

(10)   Philip believes that Tegucigalpa is in Nicaragua.

Substitution on the basis of (3) transforms (9) into the statement:

(11)   Philip is unaware that Cicero denounced Catiline,

no doubt false. Substitution on the basis of the true identity:

                    Tegucigalpa = capital of Honduras

transforms the truth (10) likewise into the falsehood:

(12)   Philip believes that the capital of Honduras is in Nicaragua.

We see therefore that the occurrences of the names 'Tully' and 'Tegucigalpa' in (9)–(10) are not purely referential.

In this there is a fundamental contrast between (9), or (10), and:

Crassus heard Tully denounce Catiline.

This statement affirms a relation between three persons, and the persons remain so related independently of the names applied to them. But (9) cannot be considered simply as affirming a relation between three persons, nor (10) a relation between person, city, and country—at least not so long as we interpret our words in such a way as to admit (9) and (10) as true and (11) and (12) as false.

Some readers may wish to construe unawareness and belief as relations between persons and statements, thus writing (9) and (10) in the manner:

(13)   Philip is unaware of 'Tully denounced Catiline',

(14)   Philip believes 'Tegucigalpa is in Nicaragua',

in order to put within a context of single quotes every not purely referential occurrence of a name. Church [5] argues against this. In so doing he exploits the concept of analyticity, concerning which we have felt misgivings (pp. 23–37 above); still his argument cannot be set lightly aside, nor are we required here to take a stand on the matter. Suffice it to say that there is certainly no *need* to reconstrue (9)–(10) in the manner (13)–(14). What *is* imperative is to observe merely that the contexts 'is unaware that . . .' and 'believes that . . .' *resemble* the context of the single quotes in this respect: a name may occur referentially in a statement S and yet not occur referentially in a longer statement which is formed by embedding S in the context 'is unaware that . . .' or 'believes that . . .'. To sum up the situation in a word, we may speak of the contexts 'is unaware that . . .' and 'believes that . . .' as *referentially opaque*.[2] The same is true of the contexts 'knows that . . .', 'says that . . .', 'doubts that

[2] This term is roughly the opposite of Russell's 'transparent' as he uses it in his Appendix C to *Principia*, 2d ed., vol. 1.

. . .', 'is surprised that . . .', etc. It would be tidy but unnecessary to force all referentially opaque contexts into the quotational mold; alternatively we can recognize quotation as one referentially opaque context among many.

It will next be shown that referential opacity afflicts also the so-called *modal* contexts 'Necessarily . . .' and 'Possibly . . .', at least when those are given the sense of *strict* necessity and possibility as in Lewis's modal logic.[3] According to the strict sense of 'necessarily' and 'possibly', these statements would be regarded as true:

(15)   9 is necessarily greater than 7,

(16)   Necessarily if there is life on the Evening Star then there is life on the Evening Star,

(17)   The number of planets is possibly less than 7,

and these as false:

(18)   The number of planets is necessarily greater than 7,

(19)   Necessarily if there is life on the Evening Star then there is life on the Morning Star,

(20)   9 is possibly less than 7.

The general idea of strict modalities is based on the putative notion of *analyticity* as follows: a statement of the form 'Necessarily . . .' is true if and only if the component statement which 'necessarily' governs is analytic, and a statement of the form 'Possibly . . .' is false if and only if the negation of the component statement which 'possibly' governs is analytic. Thus (15)–(17) could be paraphrased as follows:

(21)   '9 > 7' is analytic,

(22)   'If there is life on the Evening Star then there is life on the Evening Star' is analytic,

(23)   'The number of planets is not less than 7' is not analytic,

and correspondingly for (18)–(20).

[3] Lewis, [1], Ch. 5; Lewis and Langford, pp. 78–89, 120–166.

That the contexts 'Necessarily . . .' and 'Possibly . . .' are referentially opaque can now be quickly seen; for substitution on the basis of the true identities:

(24)   The number of planets = 9,

(25)   The Evening Star = the Morning Star

turns the truths (15)–(17) into the falsehoods (18)–(20).

Note that the fact that (15)–(17) are equivalent to (21)–(23), and the fact that '9' and 'Evening Star' and 'the number of planets' occur within quotations in (21)–(23), would not of themselves have justified us in concluding that '9' and 'Evening Star' and 'the number of planets' occur irreferentially in (15)–(17). To argue thus would be like citing the equivalence of (8) to (6) and (7) as evidence that 'Giorgione' occurs irreferentially in (8). What shows the occurrences of '9', 'Evening Star', and 'the number of planets' to be irreferential in (15)–(17) (and in (18)–(20)) is the fact that substitution by (24)–(25) turns the truths (15)–(17) into falsehoods (and the falsehoods (18)–(20) into truths).

Some, it was remarked, may like to think of (9) and (10) as receiving their more fundamental expression in (13) and (14). In the same spirit, many will like to think of (15)–(17) as receiving their more fundamental expression in (21)–(23).[4] But this again is unnecessary. We would certainly not think of (6) and (7) as somehow more basic than (8), and we need not view (21)–(23) as more basic than (15)–(17). What is important is to appreciate that the contexts 'Necessarily . . .' and 'Possibly . . .' are, like quotation and 'is unaware that . . .' and 'believes that . . .', referentially opaque.

2

The phenomenon of referential opacity has just now been explained by appeal to the behavior of singular terms. But singular terms are eliminable, we know (cf. pp. 7f, 85, 166f), by paraphrase. Ultimately the objects referred to in a theory are

---

[4] Cf. Carnap [2], pp. 245–259.

to be accounted not as the things named by the singular terms, but as the values of the variables of quantification. So, if referential opacity is an infirmity worth worrying about, it must show symptoms in connection with quantification as well as in connection with singular terms.[5] Let us then turn our attention to quantification.

The connection between naming and quantification is implicit in the operation whereby, from 'Socrates is mortal', we infer '$(\exists x)(x$ is mortal)', that is, 'Something is mortal'. This is the operation which was spoken of earlier (p. 120) as *existential generalization*, except that we now have a singular term 'Socrates' where we then had a free variable. The idea behind such inference is that whatever is true of the object named by a given singular term is true of something; and clearly the inference loses its justification when the singular term in question does not happen to name. From:

There is no such thing as Pegasus,

for example, we do not infer:

$(\exists x)$(there is no such thing as x),

that is, 'There is something which there is no such thing as', or 'There is something which there is not'.

Such inference is of course equally unwarranted in the case of an irreferential occurrence of any substantive. From (2), existential generalization would lead to:

$(\exists x)(x$ was so-called because of its size),

that is, 'Something was so-called because of its size'. This is clearly meaningless, there being no longer any suitable antecedent for 'so-called'. Note, in contrast, that existential generalization with respect to the purely referential occurrence in (5) yields the sound conclusion:

$(\exists x)(x$ was called 'Giorgione' because of its size),

that is, 'Something was called 'Giorgione' because of its size'.

---

[5] Substantially this point was made by Church [3].

The logical operation of *universal instantiation* is that whereby we infer from 'Everything is itself', for example, or in symbols '$(x)(x = x)$', the conclusion that Socrates = Socrates. This and existential generalization are two aspects of a single principle; for instead of saying that '$(x)(x = x)$' implies 'Socrates = Socrates', we could as well say that the denial 'Socrates ≠ Socrates' implies '$(\exists x)(x \neq x)$'. The principle embodied in these two operations is the link between quantifications and the singular statements that are related to them as instances. Yet it is a principle only by courtesy. It holds only in the case where a term names and, furthermore, occurs referentially. It is simply the logical content of the idea that a given occurrence is referential. The principle is, for this reason, anomalous as an adjunct to the purely logical theory of quantification. Hence the logical importance of the fact that all singular terms, aside from the variables that serve as pronouns in connection with quantifiers, are dispensable and eliminable by paraphrase.[6]

We saw just now how the referentially opaque context (2) fared under existential generalization. Let us see what happens to our other referentially opaque contexts. Applied to the occurrence of the personal name in (4), existential generalization would lead us to:

(26) $(\exists x)($'x' contains six letters$)$,

that is:

(27)   There is something such that 'it' contains six letters,

or perhaps:

(28)   'Something' contains six letters.

Now the expression:

'x' contains six letters

[6]See above, pp. 7f, 13, and below, pp. 166f. Note that existential generalization as of p. 120 does belong to pure quantification theory, for it has to do with free variables rather than singular terms. The same is true of a correlative use of universal instantiation, such as is embodied in R2 of Essay V.

means simply:

> The 24th letter of the alphabet contains six letters.

In (26) the occurrence of the letter within the context of quotes is as irrelevant to the quantifier that precedes it as is the occurrence of the same letter in the context 'six'. (26) consists merely of a falsehood preceded by an irrelevant quantifier. (27) is similar; its part:

> 'it' contains six letters

is false, and the prefix 'there is something such that' is irrelevant. (28), again, is false—if by 'contains six' we mean 'contains exactly six'.

It is less obvious, and correspondingly more important to recognize, that existential generalization is unwarranted likewise in the case of (9) and (10). Applied to (9), it leads to:

> $(\exists x)$(Philip is unaware that x denounced Catiline),

that is:

(29) Something is such that Philip is unaware that it denounced Catiline.

What is this object, that denounced Catiline without Philip's having become aware of the fact? Tully, that is, Cicero? But to suppose this would conflict with the fact that (11) is false.

Note that (29) is not to be confused with:

> Philip is unaware that $(\exists x)(x$ denounced Catiline),

which, though it happens to be false, is quite straightforward and in no danger of being inferred by existential generalization from (9).

Now the difficulty involved in the apparent consequence (29) of (9) recurs when we try to apply existential generalization to modal statements. The apparent consequences:

(30) $(\exists x)(x$ is necessarily greater than 7),

(31) $(\exists x)$(necessarily if there is life on the Evening Star then there is life on x)

of (15) and (16) raise the same questions as did (29). What is
this number which, according to (30), is necessarily greater than
7? According to (15), from which (30) was inferred, it was 9,
that is, the number of planets; but to suppose this would conflict with the fact that (18) is false. In a word, to be necessarily
greater than 7 is not a trait of a number, but depends on the manner of referring to the number. Again, what is the thing x whose
existence is affirmed in (31)? According to (16), from which (31)
was inferred, it was the Evening Star, that is, the Morning Star;
but to suppose this would conflict with the fact that (19) is false.
Being necessarily or possibly thus and so is in general not a trait
of the object concerned, but depends on the manner of referring
to the object.

Note that (30) and (31) are not to be confused with:

Necessarily $(\exists x)(x > 7)$,

Necessarily $(\exists x)$(if there is life on the Evening Star then
    there is life on x),

which present no problem of interpretation comparable to that
presented by (30) and (31). The difference may be accentuated
by a change of example: in a game of a type admitting of no tie it
is necessary that some one of the players will win, but there is
no one player of whom it may be said to be necessary that he
win.

We had seen, in the preceding section, how referential opacity manifests itself in connection with singular terms; and the
task which we then set ourselves at the beginning of this section
was to see how referential opacity manifests itself in connection
rather with variables of quantification. The answer is now apparent: if to a referentially opaque context of a variable we apply a
quantifier, with the intention that it govern that variable from
outside the referentially opaque context, then what we commonly end up with is unintended sense or nonsense of the type
(26)–(31). In a word, we cannot in general properly *quantify
into* referentially opaque contexts.

The context of quotation and the further contexts '. . . was
so called', 'is unaware that . . .', 'believes that . . .', 'Neces-

sarily . . .', and 'Possibly . . .' were found referentially opaque in the preceding section by consideration of the failure of substitutivity of identity as applied to singular terms. In the present section these contexts have been found referentially opaque by a criterion having to do no longer with singular terms, but with the miscarriage of quantification. The reader may feel, indeed, that in this second criterion we have not really got away from singular terms after all; for the discrediting of the quantifications (29)–(31) turned still on an expository interplay between the singular terms 'Tully' and 'Cicero', '9' and 'the number of planets', 'Evening Star' and 'Morning Star'. Actually, though, this expository reversion to our old singular terms is avoidable, as may now be illustrated by re-arguing the meaninglessness of (30) in another way. Whatever is greater than 7 is a number, and any given number x greater than 7 can be uniquely determined by any of various conditions, some of which have '$x > 7$' as a *necessary* consequence and some of which do not. One and the same number x is uniquely determined by the condition:

$$(32) \qquad x = \sqrt{x} + \sqrt{x} + \sqrt{x} \neq \sqrt{x}$$

and by the condition:

$$(33) \qquad \text{There are exactly } x \text{ planets,}$$

but (32) has '$x > 7$' as a necessary consequence while (33) does not. *Necessary* greaterness than 7 makes no sense as applied to a *number x;* necessity attaches only to the connection between '$x > 7$' and the particular method (32), as opposed to (33), of specifying x.

Similarly, (31) was meaningless because the sort of thing x which fulfills the condition:

(34)   If there is life on the Evening Star then there is life on x,

namely, a physical object, can be uniquely determined by any of various conditions, not all of which have (34) as a necessary consequence. *Necessary* fulfillment of (34) makes no sense as applied to a physical object x; necessity attaches, at best, only to the connection between (34) and one or another particular means of specifying x.

The importance of recognizing referential opacity is not easily overstressed. We saw in §1 that referential opacity can obstruct substitutivity of identity. We now see that it also can interrupt quantification: quantifiers outside a referentially opaque construction need have no bearing on variables inside it. This again is obvious in the case of quotation, as witness the grotesque example:

$$(\exists x)('six' \text{ contains } 'x').$$

3

We see from (30)–(31) how a quantifier applied to a modal sentence may lead simply to nonsense. Nonsense is indeed mere absence of sense, and can always be remedied by arbitrarily assigning some sense. But the important point to observe is that granted an understanding of the modalities (through uncritical acceptance, for the sake of argument, of the underlying notion of analyticity), and given an understanding of quantification ordinarily so called, we do not come out automatically with any meaning for quantified modal sentences such as (30)–(31). This point must be taken into account by anyone who undertakes to work out laws for a quantified modal logic.

The root of the trouble was the referential opacity of modal contexts. But referential opacity depends in part on the ontology accepted, that is, on what objects are admitted as possible objects of reference. This may be seen most readily by reverting for a while to the point of view of §1, where referential opacity was explained in terms of failure of interchangeability of names which name the same object. Suppose now we were to repudiate all objects which, like 9 and the planet Venus, or Evening Star, are nameable by names which fail of interchangeability in modal contexts. To do so would be to sweep away all examples indicative of the opacity of modal contexts.

But what objects would remain in a thus purified universe? An object x must, to survive, meet this condition: if S is a statement containing a referential occurrence of a name of x, and S' is formed from S by substituting any different name of x, then S and S' not only must be alike in truth value as they stand, but must stay alike in truth value even when 'necessarily' or 'possibly' is prefixed. Equivalently: putting one name of x for another in any analytic statement must yield an analytic statement. Equivalently: any two names of x must be synonymous.[7]

Thus the planet Venus as a material object is ruled out by the possession of heteronymous names 'Venus', 'Evening Star', 'Morning Star'. Corresponding to these three names we must, if modal contexts are not to be referentially opaque, recognize three objects rather than one—perhaps the Venus-concept, the Evening-Star-concept, and the Morning-Star-concept.

Similarly 9, as a unique whole number between 8 and 10, is ruled out by the possession of heteronymous names '9' and 'the number of the planets'. Corresponding to these two names we must, if modal contexts are not to be referentially opaque, recognize two objects rather than one; perhaps the 9-concept and the number-of-planets-concept. These concepts are not numbers, for the one is neither identical with nor less than nor greater than the other.

The requirement that any two names of x be synonymous might be seen as a restriction not on the admissible objects x, but on the admissible vocabulary of singular terms. So much the worse, then, for this way of phrasing the requirement; we have here simply one more manifestation of the superficiality of treating ontological questions from the vantage point of singular terms. The real insight, in danger now of being obscured, was rather this: necessity does not properly apply to the fulfillment of conditions by *objects* (such as the ball of rock which is Venus, or the number which numbers the planets), apart from special ways of specifying them. This point was most conveniently brought out by consideration of singular terms, but it is not abrogated by their elimination. Let us now review the matter from the point of view of quantification rather than singular terms.

[7] See above, p. 32. Synonymy of names does not mean merely naming the same thing; it means that the statement of identity formed of the two names is analytic.

From the point of view of quantification, the referential opacity of modal contexts was reflected in the meaninglessness of such quantifications as (30)–(31). The crux of the trouble with (30) is that a number x may be uniquely determined by each of two conditions, for example, (32) and (33), which are not necessarily, that is, analytically, equivalent to each other. But suppose now we were to repudiate all such objects and retain only objects x such that *any two conditions uniquely determining x are analytically equivalent*. All examples such as (30)–(31), illustrative of the referential opacity of modal contexts, would then be swept away. It would come to make sense in general to say that there is an object which, independently of any particular means of specifying it, is necessarily thus and so. It would become legitimate, in short, to quantify into modal contexts.

Our examples suggest no objection to quantifying into modal contexts as long as the values of any variables thus quantified are limited to *intensional objects*. This limitation would mean allowing, for purposes of such quantification anyway, not classes but only class-concepts or attributes, it being understood that two open sentences which determine the same class still determine distinct attributes unless they are analytically equivalent. It would mean allowing, for purposes of such quantification, not numbers but only some sort of concepts which are related to the numbers in a many-one way. Further it would mean allowing, for purposes of such quantification, no concrete objects but only what Frege [3] called senses of names, and Carnap [3] and Church have called individual concepts. It is a drawback of such an ontology that the principle of individuation of its entities rests invariably on the putative notion of synonymy, or analyticity.

Actually, even granted these dubious entities, we can quickly see that the expedient of limiting the values of variables to them is after all a mistaken one. It does not relieve the original difficulty over quantifying into modal contexts; on the contrary, examples quite as disturbing as the old ones can be adduced within the realm of intensional objects. For, where

A is any intensional object, say an attribute, and 'p' stands for an arbitrary true sentence, clearly

(35) $A = (\imath x)[p \, . \, (x = A)].$

Yet, if the true sentence represented by 'p' is not analytic, then neither is (35), and its sides are no more interchangeable in modal contexts than are 'Evening Star' and 'Morning Star', or '9' and 'the number of the planets'.

Or, to state the point without recourse to singular terms, it is that the requirement lately italicized—"any two conditions uniquely determining x are analytically equivalent"—is not assured merely by taking x as an intensional object. For, think of 'Fx' as any condition uniquely determining x, and think of 'p' as any nonanalytic truth. Then '$p \, . \, Fx$' uniquely determines x but is not analytically equivalent to 'Fx', even though x be an intensional object.

It was in my 1943 paper that I first objected to quantifying into modal contexts, and it was in his review of it that Church proposed the remedy of limiting the variables thus quantified to intensional values. This remedy, which I have just now represented as mistaken, seemed all right at the time. Carnap [3] adopted it in an extreme form, limiting the range of his variables to intensional objects throughout his system. He did not indeed describe his procedure thus; he complicated the picture by propounding a curious double interpretation of variables. But I have argued[8] that this complicating device has no essential bearing and is better put aside.

By the time Church came to propound an intensional logic of his own [6], he perhaps appreciated that quantification into modal contexts could not after all be legitimized simply by limiting the thus quantified variables to intensional values. Anyway his departures are more radical. Instead of a necessity operator attachable to sentences, he has a necessity predicate attachable to complex names of certain intensional objects called propositions. What makes this departure more serious than it sounds

[8] In a criticism which Carnap generously included in his [3], pp. 196f.

is that the constants and variables occurring in a sentence do not, without special provision, recur in the name of the corresponding proposition. Church makes such provision by introducing a primitive function that applies to intensional objects and yields their extensions as values. The interplay, usual in modal logic, between occurrences of expressions outside modal contexts and recurrences of them inside modal contexts, is mediated in Church's system by this function. Perhaps we should not call it a system of modal logic; Church generally did not. Anyway let my continuing discussion be understood as relating to modal logics only in the narrower sense, where the modal operator attaches to sentences.

Church [4] and Carnap tried—unsuccessfully, I have just argued—to meet my criticism of quantified modal logic by restricting the values of their variables. Arthur Smullyan took the alternative course of challenging my criticism itself. His argument depends on positing a fundamental division of names into proper names and (overt or covert) descriptions, such that proper names which name the same object are always synonymous. (Cf. (38) below.) He observes, quite rightly on these assumptions, that any examples which, like (15)–(20) and (24)–(25), show failure of substitutivity of identity in modal contexts, must exploit some descriptions rather than just proper names. Then, taking a leaf from Russell [2], he explains the failure of substitutivity by differences in the structure of the contexts, in respect of what Russell called the scopes of the descriptions.[9] As stressed in the preceding section, however, referential opacity remains to be reckoned with even when descriptions and other singular terms are eliminated altogether.

Nevertheless, the only hope of sustaining quantified modal logic lies in adopting a course that resembles Smullyan's, rather than Church [4] and Carnap [3], in this way: it must overrule my objection. It must consist in arguing or deciding that quantification into modal contexts makes sense even though any

---

[9] Unless a description fails to name, its scope is indifferent to extensional contexts. But it can still matter to intensional ones.

value of the variable of such a quantification be determinable by conditions that are not analytically equivalent to each other. The only hope lies in accepting the situation illustrated by (32) and (33) and insisting, despite it, that the object x in question is necessarily greater than 7. This means adopting an invidious attitude toward certain ways of uniquely specifying x, for example (33), and favoring other ways, for example (32), as somehow better revealing the "essence" of the object. Consequences of (32) can, from such a point of view, be looked upon as necessarily true of the object which is 9 (and is the number of the planets), while some consequences of (33) are rated still as only contingently true of that object.

Evidently this reversion to Aristotelian essentialism (cf. p. 22) is required if quantification into modal contexts is to be insisted on. An object, of itself and by whatever name or none, must be seen as having some of its traits necessarily and others contingently, despite the fact that the latter traits follow just as analytically from some ways of specifying the object as the former traits do from other ways of specifying it. In fact, we can see pretty directly that any quantified modal logic is bound to show such favoritism among the traits of an object; for surely it will be held, for each thing x, on the one hand that

(36)   necessarily $(x = x)$

and on the other hand that

(37) $\sim$ necessarily $[p \,.\, (x = x)]$,

where 'p' stands for an arbitrary contingent truth.

Essentialism is abruptly at variance with the idea, favored by Carnap, Lewis, and others, of explaining necessity by analyticity (cf. p. 143). For the appeal to analyticity can pretend to distinguish essential and accidental traits of an object only relative to how the object is specified, not absolutely. Yet the champion of quantified modal logic must settle for essentialism.

Limiting the values of his variables is neither necessary nor sufficient to justify quantifying the variables into modal contexts. Limiting their values can, however, still have this purpose in conjunction with his essentialism: if he wants to limit his essentialism to special sorts of objects, he must correspondingly limit the values of the variables which he quantifies into modal contexts.

The system presented in Miss Barcan's pioneer papers on quantified modal logic differed from the systems of Carnap and Church in imposing no special limitations on the values of variables. That she was prepared, moreover, to accept the essentialist presuppositions seems rather hinted in her theorem:

$$(38) \qquad (x)(y)\{(x = y) \supset [\text{necessarily } (x = y)]\},$$

for this is as if to say that some at least (and in fact at most; cf. 'p . Fx') of the traits that determine an object do so necessarily. The modal logic in Fitch [1] follows Miss Barcan on both points. Note incidentally that (38) follows directly from (36) and a law of substitutivity of identity for variables:

$$(x)(y)[(x = y \. Fx) \supset Fy].$$

The upshot of these reflections is meant to be that the way to do quantified modal logic, if at all, is to accept Aristotelian essentialism. To defend Aristotelian essentialism, however, is not part of my plan. Such a philosophy is as unreasonable by my lights as it is by Carnap's or Lewis's. And in conclusion I say, as Carnap and Lewis have not: so much the worse for quantified modal logic. By implication, so much the worse for unquantified modal logic as well; for, if we do not propose to quantify across the necessity operator, the use of that operator ceases to have any clear advantage over merely quoting a sentence and saying that it is analytic.

4

The worries introduced by the logical modalities are introduced also by the admission of attributes (as opposed to classes). The idiom 'the attribute of being thus and so' is referentially opaque, as may be seen, for example, from the fact that the true statement:

(39)   The attribute of exceeding 9 = the attribute of exceeding 9

goes over into the falsehood:

> The attribute of exceeding the number of the planets =
> the attribute of exceeding 9

under substitution according to the true identity (24). Moreover, existential generalization of (39) would lead to:

(40)   ($\exists x$)(the attribute of exceeding x = the attribute of exceeding 9)

which resists coherent interpretation just as did the existential generalizations (29)–(31) of (9), (15), and (16). Quantification of a sentence which contains the variable of quantification within a context of the form 'the attribute of . . .' is exactly on a par with quantification of a modal sentence.

Attributes, as remarked earlier, are individuated by this principle: two open sentences which determine the same class do not determine the same attribute unless they are analytically equivalent. Now another popular sort of intensional entity is the *proposition*. Propositions are conceived in relation to statements as attributes are conceived in relation to open sentences: two statements determine the same proposition just in case they are analytically equivalent. The foregoing strictures on attributes obviously apply equally to propositions. The truth:

(41)   The proposition that 9 > 7 = the proposition that 9 > 7

goes over into the falsehood:

> The proposition that the number of the planets > 7 = the
> proposition that 9 > 7.

under substitution according to (24). Existential generalization of (41) yields a result comparable to (29)–(31) and (40).

Most of the logicians, semanticists, and analytical philosophers who discourse freely of attributes, propositions, or logical modalities betray failure to appreciate that they thereby imply a metaphysical position which they themselves would scarcely condone. It is noteworthy that in *Principia Mathematica*, where attributes were nominally admitted as entities, all actual con-

texts occurring in the course of formal work are such as could
be fulfilled as well by classes as by attributes. All actual contexts
are *extensional* in the sense of page 30 above. The authors of
Principia Mathematica thus adhered in practice to a principle
of extensionality which they did not espouse in theory. If their
practice had been otherwise, we might have been brought sooner
to an appreciation of the urgency of the principle.

We have seen how modal sentences, attribute terms, and
proposition terms conflict with the nonessentialist view of the
universe. It must be kept in mind that those expressions create
such conflict only when they are quantified into, that is, when
they are put under a quantifier and themselves contain the variable of quantification. We are familiar with the fact (illustrated
by (26) above) that a quotation cannot contain an effectively free
variable, reachable by an outside quantifier. If we preserve a
similar attitude toward modalities, attribute terms, and proposition terms, we may then make free use of them without any misgivings of the present urgent kind.

What has been said of modality in these pages relates only
to strict modality. For other sorts, for example, physical necessity and possibility, the first problem would be to formulate
the notions clearly and exactly. Afterward we could investigate
whether such modalities, like the strict ones, cannot be quantified into without precipitating an ontological crisis. The question concerns intimately the practical use of language. It concerns, for example, the use of the contrary-to-fact conditional
within a quantification; for it is reasonable to suppose that the
contrary-to-fact conditional reduces to the form 'Necessarily, if
p then q' in some sense of necessity. Upon the contrary-to-
fact conditional depends in turn, for example, this definition of
solubility in water: To say that an object is soluble in water is
to say that it would dissolve if it were in water. In discussions
of physics, naturally, we need quantifications containing the
clause 'x is soluble in water', or the equivalent in words; but,
according to the definition suggested, we should then have to
admit within quantifications the expression 'if x were in water
then x would dissolve', that is, 'necessarily if x is in water then

x dissolves'. Yet we do not know whether there is a suitable sense of 'necessarily' into which we can so quantify.[10]

Any way of imbedding statements within statements, whether based on some notion of "necessity" or, for example, on a notion of "probability" as in Reichenbach, must be carefully examined in relation to its susceptibility to quantification. Perhaps the only useful modes of statement composition susceptible to unrestricted quantification are the truth functions. Happily, no other mode of statement composition is needed, at any rate, in mathematics; and mathematics, significantly, is the branch of science whose needs are most clearly understood.

Let us return, for a final sweeping observation, to our first test of referential opacity, namely, failure of substitutivity of identity; and let us suppose that we are dealing with a theory in which (a) *logically* equivalent formulas are interchangeable in all contexts *salva veritate* and (b) the logic of classes is at hand.[11] For such a theory it can be shown that *any* mode of statement composition, other than the truth functions, is referentially opaque. For, let ϕ and ψ be any statements alike in truth value, and let $\Phi(\phi)$ be any true statement containing ϕ as a part. What is to be shown is that $\Phi(\psi)$ will also be true, unless the context represented by 'Φ' is referentially opaque. Now the class named by $\hat{a}\phi$ is either V or Λ, according as ϕ is true or false; for remember that ϕ is a statement, devoid of free a. (If the notation $\hat{a}\phi$ without recurrence of a seems puzzling, read it as $\hat{a}(a = a \,.\, \phi)$.) Moreover ϕ is logically equivalent to $\hat{a}\phi = $ V. Hence, by (a), since $\Phi(\phi)$ is true, so is $\Phi(\hat{a}\phi = $ V). But $\hat{a}\phi$ and $\hat{a}\psi$ name one and the same class, since ϕ and ψ are alike in truth value. Then, since $\Phi(\hat{a}\phi = $ V) is true, so is $\Phi(\hat{a}\psi = $ V) unless the context represented by 'Φ' is referentially opaque. But if $\Phi(\hat{a}\psi = $ V) is true, then so in turn is $\Phi(\psi)$, by (a).

[10] For a theory of disposition terms, like 'soluble', see Carnap [5].
[11] See above, pp. 27, 87.

IX
MEANING AND EXISTENTIAL INFERENCE

Topics dealt with in earlier pages include logical truth, singular terms, and the distinction between meaning and reference. In the present pages, illustrative in purpose, we shall see how several curiously interrelated perplexities that have arisen in the literature are traceable to difficulty over those three topics.

1

It has frequently been claimed[1] that though the schemata:

$$(1) \quad (\exists x)(Fx \lor \sim Fx), \qquad (2) \quad (x)Fx \supset (\exists x)Fx$$

are demonstrable in quantification theory, the statements of the forms which these schemata depict are not logically true. For, it is argued, such statements depend for their truth upon there being something in the universe; and that there is something is, though true, not logically true.

The argument is right in its first premiss: the described statements do indeed depend for their truth upon there being something. But the rest of the argument turns on an obscure standard of logical truth, for clearly any statements of the forms (1) and (2) *are* logically true according to the definition of logical truth given above.[2] Those who protest that such statements are not logically true would protest also—without perhaps distinguishing the two protests—that the statements are not

---

[1] For example, by Russell [1], note to Ch. 18; Langford [1]; von Wright, p. 20.
[2] Pp. 22f.

analytic. Therewith the notion of analyticity is pushed into yet deeper obscurity than seemed to envelope it on last consideration;[3] for it seemed at that time that one class of statements that could clearly be included under the head of analytic statements was the class of the logical truths in the sense of the mentioned definition.

The widespread misgivings as to the logical truth or analyticity of statements of the forms (1) and (2) will evidently have to be left in the following vague shape: analyticity is, vaguely, truth by virtue of meanings; meanings of words do not legislate regarding existence; therefore the statements in question are not analytic. The issue is a representative issue of the theory of meaning.

But those who object to so fashioning quantification theory as to include (1) and (2) as logical theorems betray lack of appreciation of an important technical point. The following fact is demonstrable regarding quantificational schemata: those which turn out valid for all choices of universe of a given size also turn out valid for all smaller universes, except for the empty one.[4] This means that if in formulating the laws of quantification theory we disregard universes of, say, one to ten objects, in hopes of putting further laws at our disposal which will be useful for seriously large universes, we meet with frustration; there are no further laws, not holding also for universes of size one to ten. But with the empty universe the situation is very different: laws, for example, (1) and (2), fail for it which hold for all larger universes. It behooves us therefore to put aside the one relatively inutile case of the empty universe, so as not to cut ourselves off from laws applicable in all other cases. It behooves us the more because it is always particularly easy to make a separate test to decide, if we like, whether a given theorem of quantification theory (valid for all nonempty universes) holds or fails for the empty universe; we have merely to mark all the universal quantifications as true and all the existential ones as false, and see whether our theorem then comes out true or false.

[3] Pp. 23–37.
[4] See, for example, my [2], p. 97.

The existence of this supplementary test shows incidentally that there is no difficulty whatever in so framing quantification theory as to exclude theorems such as (1) and (2) which fail for the empty universe; but from the point of view of utility in application it would be folly, as we have seen, to want to limit the laws of quantification theory in this way.

The moral of the foregoing paragraph holds even if we honor the misgivings described in the paragraph before it. He who entertains those misgivings has simply to view the theorems of quantification theory not as logically valid, but as logically implied by schemata such as (1) and (2). Quantification theory then retains its present form and its present utility and even its status as a purely logical discipline; we have merely shifted the logical characterization of theoremhood.

2

We turn now to a derivative problem. Langford has argued ([2], [3]) that the singular statements '*Fa*' and '*~Fa*', where '*F*' is thought of now as some specific predicate (rather than a schematic letter) and '*a*' as a name, cannot be mutual contradictories. For each of them has the logical consequence '*Fa* **v** *~Fa*', which in turn has the logical consequence (1). Since (1) is not logically true, he argues, and mutual contradictories cannot share any logical consequences except logical truths, it follows that '*Fa*' and '*~Fa*' are not really contradictories.

One is tempted to dismiss the argument by saying that the absurdity of the conclusion simply goes to discredit a too narrow notion of logical truth, and to sustain our broader version of logical truth which counts statements of the form (1) as logically true. But to argue thus would be to overlook, and perpetuate, the more basic fault in Langford's argument, namely, the assertion that '*Fa* **v** *~Fa*' logically implies (1). We who view (1) as logically true would of course concede that (1) is logically implied by anything; but he cannot. For him the step from '*Fa* **v** *~Fa*' to (1) must depend specifically on existential generalization.[5] But for inference of this type we know no defense save on the

[5] See above, pp. 145f.

assumption that 'a' names something, that is, that a exists; hence '$Fa \lor {\sim}Fa$' could scarcely be said to imply (1) *logically*, for Langford, unless it were logically true that a exists. But if it were logically true that a exists, it would be logically true that there is something; hence any statement of the form (1) would be logically true after all.

Langford also has another argument, not involving (1), to show that 'Fa' and '${\sim}Fa$' are not contradictories, namely, that each of them analytically implies 'a exists', and 'a exists' is not analytic. But in this argument the questionable assertion is that each of 'Fa' and '${\sim}Fa$' implies 'a exists'.

The notion that 'Fa' (and '${\sim}Fa$') implies 'a exists' arises from the notion that 'Fa' has as its "meaning" a certain proposition[6] whose constituents are the meanings of 'F' and 'a'. If 'Fa' is meaningful, it is reasoned, then this proposition must exist, and hence so must its constituent a. But if 'Fa' or '${\sim}Fa$' is true then 'Fa' is meaningful and consequently a exists. Now the flaw in this reasoning is quickly picked out even if we grant the bizarre apparatus of propositions and constituents, namely, existence of the meaning of 'a' was confused with existence of a. The confusion is the familiar switch of meaning with naming.

But if the faulty reasoning last noted is stopped in the middle, short of where the fallacy occurred, we still have an argument which bears scrutiny—an argument from 'Fa' (or '${\sim}Fa$') not to the existence of a, but to the existence of the proposition which is the meaning of 'Fa'. If that proposition exists then something exists, and then (1) holds; so we seem to have a new argument to show that each of 'Fa' and '${\sim}Fa$' analytically implies, not indeed 'a exists', but (1).

In full, the chain of deduction which we are now imagining is as follows: if Fa (or ${\sim}Fa$) then 'Fa' (or '${\sim}Fa$') is true; then 'Fa' is meaningful; then the meaning of 'Fa' exists; then there is something; then $(\exists x)(Fx \lor {\sim}Fx)$. Each link of the chain must hold as an analytic implication, if the argument is to show that each of 'Fa' and '${\sim}Fa$' implies (1). But one might doubt that meaningfulness of 'Fa' analytically implies that the mean-

[6] See above, pp. 108f, 156f.

ing of '*Fa*' exists; it will be recalled that the notion of meanings as entities seemed rather more dubious than the notion of meaningfulness.[7] Also, as noted by Lewy and White [1], it may be doubted that the first link, connecting '*Fa*' with "'*Fa*' is true' (and '~*Fa*' with "'~*Fa*' is true'), should be regarded as analytic. We cannot assess the links of the chain with much confidence, for the chain is imbedded in the muddiest stretch of a very muddy field, the theory of meaning.

Langford's problem has had a further noteworthy ramification in the literature. Referring to Langford's claim that '*Fa*' and '~*Fa*' share the consequence '*a* exists', Nelson writes that we might with equal justice argue that they share the consequence '*F* exists', and even that '$(x)Fx$' and '~$(x)Fx$' share the consequence '*F* exists', and even that '*p*' and '~*p*' share the consequence '*p* exists'. Thus, he observes, we might with equal justice conclude that there are no contradictories at all in logic.

Nelson's phrase "with equal justice" disarms direct opposition. I would note only that we have here a museum specimen of what was inveighed against earlier—the treatment of general terms and statements as names, or, what comes to the same thing, the treatment of schematic letters as variables.[8]

Actually Nelson does not accept the conclusion that there are no contradictories in logic. He undertakes to obviate it, and also Langford's weaker conclusion, by proposing a distinction between "implies" and "presupposes"—a subtle distinction which I shall not attempt to evaluate, since we seem anyway to have found our way through the problems which occasioned it.

3

We freed ourselves, six paragraphs back, of any general constraint to admit the inference of '*a* exists' from '*Fa*' and '~*Fa*'. We are led to wonder, however, just what statements containing '*a*' *should* be regarded as requiring for their truth that *a* exist.

Under ordinary usage, truth values seem to attach to singular

[7] See above, pp. 11f, 22, 48.
[8] See above, pp. 108–116.

statements only conditionally upon existence of the named object. There are exceptions; certainly 'Pegasus exists' and '~Pegasus exists' are fixed in point of truth value, namely, as respectively false and true, by the very nonexistence of Pegasus. But there would seem, under ordinary usage, to be no way of adjudicating the truth values of 'Pegasus flies' and '~Pegasus flies'; the nonexistence of Pegasus seems to dispose of the question without answering it. The case is analogous to that of conditional statements: discovery of the falsity of the antecedent of a conditional in the indicative mood seems from the standpoint of ordinary usage to dispose of the question of the truth value of the conditional without answering it.

Logic, however, presumes to a certain creativity which sets it apart from philology. Logic seeks to systematize, as simply as possible, the rules for moving from truths to truths; and if the system can be simplified by some departure from past linguistic usage which does not interfere with the utility of language as a tool of science, the logician does not hesitate to proclaim the departure. One way in which simplicity has been gained is by doing away with quirks of usage of the kind noted in the preceding paragraph, so as to endow every statement with a truth value. Thus it is that the indicative conditional of ordinary language has given way in the logically regimented language of science to the material conditional, which, while serving still the scientific purposes of the old, does not share the defectiveness of the old with regard to truth values. The material conditional formed from any two statements has a definite truth value; discovery of the falsity of the antecedent of a material conditional disposes of the question of the truth value of the conditional not by dismissing it, but by delivering the answer "true". Now the defectiveness of singular statements in point of truth values calls, in the interests of simplicity of logical rules, for a similar revision on the logician's part—a supplementation of ordinary usage by assigning truth values to those singular statements which, by ordinary usage, have lacked them.

Just how to make these supplementary assignments is an arbitrary matter, to be decided by convenience. Convenience obviously demands above all that the assignments not be such as to create exceptions to the existing laws governing truth-functional compounds and quantification. It behooves us therefore to make our arbitrary assignments only to atomic singular statements, and then to let the truth values of compounds be determined from those of their components by existing logical laws.

So the question comes down to this: what truth value shall we give an atomic singular statement when it does not have a determinate truth value by ordinary usage? The indeterminate atomic singular statements concerned are most of those whose singular terms fail to name; the exceptions which are determinate are '*a* exists' and any others to the same or opposite effect. Now we can make the assignment arbitrarily; let us say they are all to be false. In so choosing we have taken our cue from the determinate example '*a* exists', which of course is false if '*a*' fails to name.

Such, though he spared us the philosophical background which I have here sketched in, was Chadwick's answer to Langford. '*Fa*' and '~*Fa*' do of course become contradictories under the described procedure. Existential generalization, if performed independently of supplementary information as to existence of the named object, comes to be dependable in general only in case the singular statement from which the inference is made is atomic. Langford remains right in inferring '*a* exists' from an atomic premiss '*Fa*', but not in inferring it also from '~*Fa*'.

The treatment which we have accorded to singular statements whose singular terms fail to name is admittedly artificial, but, we saw, amply motivated independently of Langford's problem. It has a precedent, by the way, in the logical theory of descriptions. The contextual definition of description given above,[9] which is a simplified version of Russell's, is readily seen to have the effect of making the atomic contexts of a description false when the described object does not exist. This is not to say that the foregoing treatment of singular terms is less artificial

[9] P. 85. The only primitive predicate there was 'ϵ', but we may add analogues of D9–10 corresponding to any given extralogical predicates.

than it seemed, but that the theory of descriptions is equally so. But the artifice is in each case a good one. The logical nature and value of the artifice in the case of descriptions can be made out in the same way as was done in foregoing paragraphs for the case of singular terms; indeed, the one case includes the other, for descriptions are singular terms.

In fact, the two cases coincide if we take the further step, remarked on earlier,[10] of reconstruing proper names trivially as descriptions. The theoretical advantages of so doing are overwhelming. The whole category of singular terms is thereby swept away, so far as theory is concerned; for we know how to eliminate descriptions. In dispensing with the category of singular terms we dispense with a major source of theoretical confusion, to instances of which I have called attention in the present essay and in the discussions of ontological commitment in preceding essays. In particular, we dispense altogether, in theory, with the perplexing form of notation 'a exists'; for we know how to translate singular existence statements into more basic logical terms when the singular term involved is a description.[11] Furthermore, the rules of inference by existential generalization and universal instantiation, in the anomalous form in which they have to do with singular terms,[12] are reduced to the status of derivable rules and thus eliminated from the theoretical foundations of logic.

[10] Pp. 7f.
[11] See above, p. 7.
[12] See above, p. 146.

ORIGINS OF THE ESSAYS

"On what there is" appeared in the *Review of Metaphysics* in 1948, earlier versions having been presented as lectures at Princeton and Yale in March and May of that year. It lent its title to a symposium at the joint session of the Aristotelian Society and the Mind Association at Edinburgh, July 1951, and was reprinted, along with the animadversions of the symposiasts, in the Aristotelian Society's supplementary volume *Freedom, Language, and Reality* (London: Harrison, 1951). It is reprinted also in Linsky's anthology. The changes occurring in the present version are mostly confined to footnotes.

"Two dogmas of empiricism" appeared in the *Philosophical Review* in January 1951, having been read, with omissions, to the Eastern Division of the American Philosophical Association in December 1950 at Toronto. In May 1951 it became the subject of a symposium of the Institute for the Unity of Science in Boston and also of a meeting at Stanford University, for which occasion it was reissued by mimeograph. The version printed here diverges from the original in footnotes and in other minor respects: §§1 and 6 have been abridged where they encroach on the preceding essay, and §§3–4 have been expanded at points.

"The problem of meaning in linguistics" is the text, abridged in some portions and expanded in others, of a lecture given in the Linguistics Forum at Ann Arbor in August 1951.

"Identity, ostension, and hypostasis" appeared in the *Journal of Philosophy* in 1950. It was drawn in large part from the Theodore and Grace de Laguna Lecture, "Identity," which I gave at Bryn Mawr in December 1949, and in smaller part from a lecture "On ontologies" which I gave at the University of Southern California in July 1949. The essay is reprinted here almost unchanged except in the references.

"New foundations for mathematical logic" appeared in the *American Mathematical Monthly* in February 1937, having been read to the Mathematical Association of America in December 1936 at Chapel Hill, North Carolina. The paper as reprinted here departs from the original only in annotation, correction of several errors, and small changes of notation and terminology. But the material headed "Supplementary remarks" is wholly foreign to the original. The first part of this material is the gist of the first part of my "Logic based on inclusion and abstraction," *Journal of Symbolic Logic*, 1937. The rest is newly written.

"Logic and the reification of universals" derives mainly from a paper "On the problem of universals" which I read to the Association for Symbolic Logic, February 1947, in New York. Part of that paper came into print as part of an article "On universals," *Journal of Symbolic Logic*, 1947, but the present essay draws also on the unpublished part. It draws also on two other papers: "Semantics and abstract objects" (*Proceedings of the American Academy of Arts and Sciences*, 1951), which was read in Boston at the April 1950 meeting of the Institute for the Unity of Science, and "Designation and existence" (*Journal of Philosophy*, 1939; reprinted in Feigl and Sellars), which was an abridgment of a paper read in Cambridge, Massachusetts, at the September 1939 Congress for the Unity of Science.

"Notes on the theory of reference" is partly new, partly drawn from the aforementioned paper "Semantics and abstract objects," and partly drawn from "Ontology and ideology," *Philosophical Studies*, 1951.

"Reference and modality" has grown out of a fusion of "Notes on existence and necessity," *Journal of Philosophy*, 1943, with "The problem of interpreting modal logic," *Journal of Symbolic Logic*, 1947. Sundry omissions, revisions, and insertions have been made. The parent article "Notes on existence and necessity" is reprinted in Linsky. It was in the main a translation in turn of portions of my book *O Sentido da nova lógica* (São Paulo, Brazil: Livraria Martins, 1944), which embodied a course of lectures delivered at São Paulo in 1942.

"Meaning and existential inference" is newly written, but the points in it derive mostly from my review of E. J. Nelson in the *Journal of Symbolic Logic*, 1947.

BIBLIOGRAPHICAL REFERENCES

Ackermann and Hilbert, *see* Hilbert.

Barcan, R. C., "A functional calculus based on strict implication," *Journal of Symbolic Logic 11* (1946), 1–16.

——— "The identity of individuals in a strict functional calculus of second order," *ibid. 12* (1947), 12–15. See correction of my review, *ibid. 23* (1958), 342.

Bernays, Paul [1], "Sur le platonisme dans les mathématiques," *L'Enseignement mathématique 34* (1935–36), 52–69.

——— [2], "A system of axiomatic set theory," *Journal of Symbolic Logic 2* (1937), 65–77; *6* (1941), 1–17; *7* (1942), 65–89; 133–145; *8* (1943), 89–106; *13* (1948), 65–79.

——— and Hilbert, *see* Hilbert.

Black, Max, *The Nature of Mathematics* (London: Kegan Paul, 1933; New York: Harcourt Brace, 1934).

Bloch, Bernard, and G. L. Trager, *Outline of Linguistic Analysis* (Baltimore: Linguistic Society of America, 1942).

Bloomfield, Leonard, *Language* (New York: Holt, 1933).

Brouwer, L. E. J. "Consciousness, philosophy, and mathematics," *Proceedings of 10th International Congress of Philosophy* (Amsterdam, 1949), pp. 1235–1249.

Bühler, Karl, "Phonetik und Phonologie," *Travaux du Cercle Linguistique de Prague 4* (1931), 22–53. (Especially p. 32.)

Cantor, Georg, "Ueber eine elementare Frage der Mannigfaltigkeitslehre," *Jahresberichte der deutschen Mathematiker-Vereinigungen 1* (1890–91), 75–78. Reprinted in *Gesammelte Abhandlungen* (Berlin, 1932).

Carnap, Rudolf [1], *Der logische Aufbau der Welt* (Berlin, 1928).

——— [2], *The Logical Syntax of Language* (New York: Harcourt Brace, and London: Kegan Paul, 1937). Translation, with extensions, of *Logische Syntax der Sprache* (Vienna: Springer, 1934).

171

—— [3], *Meaning and Necessity* (Chicago: University of Chicago Press, 1947).

—— [4], *Logical Foundations of Probability* (Chicago: University of Chicago Press, 1950).

—— [5], "Testability and meaning," *Philosophy of Science 3* (1936), 419–471; *4* (1937), 1–40 (reprinted, New Haven: Graduate Philosophy Club, Yale University, 1950).

—— [6], "Empiricism, semantics, and ontology," *Revue internationale de philosophie 4* (1950), 20–40. Reprinted in Linsky.

Cassirer, Ernst, *Language and Myth* (New York: Harper, 1946). Translation of *Sprache und Mythos* (Berlin, 1925).

Chadwick, J. A., "On propositions belonging to logic," *Mind 36* (1927), 347–353.

Church, Alonzo [1], "A set of postulates for the foundation of logic," *Annals of Mathematics 33* (1932), 346–366; *34* (1933), 839–864.

—— [2], "A note on the Entscheidungsproblem," *Journal of Symbolic Logic 1* (1936), 40f, 101f. (For a possibly more convenient presentation of the argument, see Hilbert and Bernays, vol. 2, pp. 416–421.)

—— [3], Review of Quine, *ibid. 7* (1942), 100f.

—— [4], Review of Quine, *ibid. 8* (1943), 45ff.

—— [5], "On Carnap's analysis of statements of assertion and belief," *Analysis 10* (1950), 97ff.

—— [6], "A formulation of the logic of sense and denotation," in *Structure, Method, and Meaning: Essays in Honor of Henry M. Sheffer* (Paul Henle, H. M. Kallen, and S. K. Langer, eds.; New York: Liberal Arts Press, 1951), pp. 3–24.

—— and W. V. Quine, "Some theorems on definability and decidability," *Journal of Symbolic Logic 17* (1952), pp. 179–187.

Curry, H. B. "A simplification of the theory of combinators," *Synthèse 7* (1948–49), 391–399. (Contains further references.)

Duhem, Pierre, *La Théorie physique: son objet et sa structure* (Paris, 1906).

Feigl, Herbert, and Wilfrid Sellars (eds.), *Readings in Philosophical Analysis* (New York: Appleton-Century-Crofts, 1949).

Fitch, F. B. [1], *Symbolic Logic* (New York: Ronald Press, 1952).

—— [2], "The consistency of the ramified Principia," *Journal of Symbolic Logic 3* (1938), 140–149.

—— [3], "The problem of the Morning Star and the Evening Star," *Philosophy of Science 16* (1949), 137–141.

Fraenkel, A. A., "Sur la notion d'existence dans les mathématiques," *L'Enseignement mathématique 34* (1935–36), 18–32.

Frank, Philipp, *Modern Science and its Philosophy* (Cambridge: Harvard University Press, 1949).

Frege, Gottlob [1], *Foundations of Arithmetic* (New York: Philosophical Library, 1950). Reprint of *Grundlagen der Arithmetik* (Breslau, 1884) with English translation in parallel.

—— [2], *Grundgesetze der Arithmetik*, 2 vols. (Jena, 1893, 1903).

—— [3], "On sense and nominatum," in Feigl and Sellars, pp. 85–102. Translation of "Ueber Sinn und Bedeutung," *Zeitschrift für Philosophie und philosophische Kritik 100* (1892), 25–50.

Gödel, Kurt [1], "Die Vollständigkeit der Axiome des logischen Funktionenkalküls, *Monatshefte für Mathematik und Physik 37* (1930), 349–360. (For a simpler proof of this result, see Henkin.)

—— [2], "Ueber formal unentscheidbare Sätze der Principia Mathematica und verwandter Systeme," *ibid. 38* (1931), 173–198. (For an introductory account and further references see Quine [2], pp. 245ff.)

Goodman, Nelson, *The Structure of Appearance* (Cambridge: Harvard University Press, 1951).

—— and W. V. Quine, "Steps toward a constructive nominalism," *Journal of Symbolic Logic 12* (1947), 105–122. (Lest the reader be led to misconstrue passages in the present book by trying to reconcile them with the appealingly forthright opening sentence of the cited paper, let me say that I should now prefer to treat that sentence as a hypothetical statement of conditions for the construction in hand.)

Grelling, Kurt, and Leonard Nelson, "Bemerkungen zu den Paradoxien von Russell and Burali-Forti," *Abhandlungen der Fries'schen Schule 2* (1907–8), 300–334.

Hahn, Hans, *Ueberflüssige Wesenheiten* (Vienna, 1930).

Hailperin, Theodore, "A set of axioms for logic," *Journal of Symbolic Logic 9* (1944), 1–19.

Hempel, C. G. [1], "Problems and changes in the empiricist criterion of meaning," *Revue internationale de philosophie 4* (1950), 41–63. Reprinted in Linsky.

—— [2], "The concept of cognitive significance: a reconsideration," *Proceedings of American Academy of Arts and Sciences 80* (1951), 61–77.

Henkin, Leon, "The completeness of the first-order functional calculus," *Journal of Symbolic Logic 14* (1949), 159–166.

Heyting, Arend, *Mathematische Grundlagenforschung, Intuitionismus, Beweistheorie* (Berlin: Springer, 1934).

Hilbert, David, and Wilhelm Ackermann, *Grundzüge der theoretischen Logik* (Berlin: Springer, 1928, 1938, 1949). English version of 1938 edition: *Principles of Mathematical Logic* (New York: Chelsea, 1950).

—— and Paul Bernays, *Grundlagen der Mathematik*. 2 vols. (Berlin: Springer, 1934, 1939; 2d printing, Ann Arbor: Edwards, 1944).

Hume, David, *A Treatise of Human Nature.* (Especially Book 1, Part 4, Section 2.)

Kleene, S. C., and Barkley Rosser, "The inconsistency of certain formal logics," *Annals of Mathematics 36* (1935), 630–636.

Kuratowski, Casimir, "Sur la notion de l'ordre dans la théorie des ensembles," *Fundamenta Mathematicae 2* (1921), 161–171.

Langford, C. H. [1], "On propositions belonging to logic," *Mind 36* (1927), 342–346.

———— [2], "Singular propositions," *ibid. 37* (1928), 73–81.

———— [3], "Propositions directly about particulars," *ibid. 38* (1929), 219–225.

———— and Lewis, *see* Lewis.

Lewis, C. I. [1], *A Survey of Symbolic Logic* (Berkeley, 1918).

———— [2], *An Analysis of Knowledge and Valuation* (LaSalle, Ill.: Open Court, 1946).

———— and C. H. Langford, *Symbolic Logic* (New York, 1932; 2d printing, New York: Dover, 1951).

Lewy, Casimir, "Truth and significance," *Analysis 8* (1947), 24–27.

Linsky, Leonard (ed.), *Semantics and the Philosophy of Language* (Urbana: University of Illinois Press, 1952).

Lowinger, Armand, *The Methodology of Pierre Duhem* (New York: Columbia University Press, 1941).

Łukasiewicz, Jan, "Uwagi o aksyomacie Nicod'a i o 'dedukcyi uogólniającej'," *Księga pamiątkowa Polskiego Towarzystwa Filozoficznego we Lwowie* (Lwów, 1931).

Martin, R. M., "On 'analytic'," *Philosophical Studies 3* (1952), 42–47.

Meyerson, Émile, *Identité et realité* (Paris, 1908; 4th ed., 1932).

Mostowski, Andrzej, "Some impredicative definitions in the axiomatic set theory," *Fundamenta Mathematicae 37* (1950), 111–124.

Myhill, J. R., "A complete theory of natural, rational, and real numbers," *Journal of Symbolic Logic 15* (1950), 185–196.

Nelson, E. J., "Contradiction and the presupposition of existence," *Mind 55* (1946), 319–327.

Neumann, J. von, "Eine Axiomatisierung der Mengenlehre," *Journal für reine und angewandte Mathematik 154* (1925), 219–240; *155* (1926), 128.

Nicod, Jean, "A reduction in the number of primitive propositions of logic," *Proceedings of Cambridge Philosophical Society 19* (1917–20), 32–41. (See also Quine, "A note on Nicod's postulate," *Mind 41* (1932), 345–350.)

Peano, Giuseppe, "Sulla definizione di funzione," *Atti della Reale Accademia dei Lincei,* rendiconti, classe di scienze, *20* (1911), 3ff.

Pike, K. L., *Phonemics: A Technique for Reducing Languages to Writing* (Ann Arbor: University of Michigan Press, 1947).

Poincaré, Henri, *Sechs Vorträge über ausgewählte Gegenstände aus der reinen Mathematik und mathematischen Physik* (Leipzig and Berlin, 1910).

Quine, W. V. [1], *Mathematical Logic* (New York: Norton, 1940; Cambridge: Harvard University Press, 1947; rev. ed., Cambridge: Harvard University Press, 1951).

———— [2], *Methods of Logic* (New York: Holt, 1950).

———— [3], "On the axiom of reducibility," *Mind 45* (1936), 498ff.

———— [4], "On Cantor's theorem," *Journal of Symbolic Logic 2* (1937), 120–124.

———— [5], "Logic based on inclusion and abstraction," *ibid.*, 145–152.

———— [6], "On the theory of types," *ibid. 3* (1938), 125–139.

———— [7], "On ω-inconsistency and a so-called axiom of infinity," *ibid. 18* (1953).

———— [8], "On an application of Tarski's theory of truth," *Proceedings of National Academy of Sciences 38* (1952), 430–433.

———— and Church, *see* Church; and Goodman, *see* Goodman.

Reichenbach, Hans, *The Theory of Probability* (Berkeley and Los Angeles: University of California Press, 1949). Translation, with revisions, of *Wahrscheinlichkeitslehre* (Leyden: Sijthoff, 1935).

Robinson, Julia, "Definability and decision problems in arithmetic," *Journal of Symbolic Logic 14* (1949), 98–114.

Rosser, Barkley, "The Burali-Forti paradox," *Journal of Symbolic Logic 7* (1942), 1–17.

———— and Kleene, *see* Kleene.

Russell, Bertrand [1], *Introduction to Mathematical Philosophy* (London, 1919, 1920).

BIBLIOGRAPHICAL REFERENCES 177

———— [2], "On denoting," *Mind 14* (1905), 479–493. Reprinted in Feigl and Sellars.

———— [3], "Mathematical logic as based on the theory of types," *American Journal of Mathematics 30* (1908), 222–262.

———— [4], "The philosophy of logical atomism," *Monist 28* (1918), 495–527; *29* (1919), 32–63, 190–222, 345–380. (Reprinted, Minneapolis: Department of Philosophy, University of Minnesota, 1949).

———— and Whitehead, *see* Whitehead.

Schönfinkel, Moses, "Ueber die Bausteine der mathematischen Logik," *Mathematische Annalen 92* (1924), 305–316.

Smullyan, A. F., "Modality and description," *Journal of Symbolic Logic 13* (1948), 31–37. *See also* Fitch [3].

Tarski, Alfred [1], *A Decision Method for Elementary Algebra and Geometry* (Santa Monica: Rand Corporation, 1948; rev. ed., Berkeley and Los Angeles: University of California Press, 1951).

———— [2], "Sur les *truth-functions* au sens de MM. Russell et Whitehead," *Fundamenta Mathematicae 5* (1924), 59–74.

———— [3], "Einige methodologische Untersuchungen über die Definierbarkeit der Begriffe," *Erkenntnis 5* (1935–36), 80–100.

———— [4], "Der Wahrheitsbegriff in den formalisierten Sprachen," *Studia Philosophica 1* (1936), 261–405.

———— [5], "On undecidable statements in enlarged systems of logic and the concept of truth," *Journal of Symbolic Logic 4* (1939), 105–112.

———— [6], "The semantic conception of truth and the foundations of semantics," *Philosophy and Phenomenological Research 4* (1944), 341–376. Reprinted in Feigl and Sellars; also in Linsky.

Thomson, J. F., "A note on truth," *Analysis 9* (1949), 67–72; *10* (1949), 23–24.

Tooke, J. H. Ἔπεα πτερόεντα; *or, The Diversions of Purley.* 2 vols. (London, 1786, 1805, 1829; Boston, 1806).

Trager and Bloch, *see* Bloch.

Wang, Hao, "A formal system of logic," *Journal of Symbolic Logic 15* (1950), 25–32.

Weyl, Hermann, *Das Kontinuum* (Leipzig, 1918, 1932).

White, Morton [1], Review of Lewy, *Journal of Symbolic Logic 13* (1948), 125f.

——— [2], "The analytic and the synthetic: an untenable dualism," in Sidney Hook (ed.), *John Dewey: Philosopher of Science and Freedom* (New York: Dial Press, 1950), pp. 316–330. Reprinted in Linsky.

Whitehead, A. N., and Bertrand Russell, *Principia Mathematica.* 3 vols. (Cambridge, England, 1910–1913; 2d ed., 1925–1927).

Whorf, B. L., "Time, space and language," in Laura Thompson, *Culture in Crisis* (New York: Harper, 1950), pp. 152–172.

Wiener, Norbert, "A simplification of the logic of relations," *Proceedings of Cambridge Philosophical Society 17* (1912–14), 387–390.

Wright, G. H. von, "On the idea of logical truth (I)," *Societas Scientiarum Fennica, Commentationes Physico-Mathematicae 14* (1948), no. 4.

Zermelo, Ernst, "Untersuchungen über die Grundlagen der Mengenlehre," *Mathematische Annalen 65* (1908), 261–281.

INDEX

Abstract: algebra 81; entities 3n, 45, 73; terms 21, 30, 76, 78. *See also* Attribute, Class, Name

Abstraction: of attributes 76, 156; of classes 30, 76ff, 87, 94ff, 104, 159; of functions 104; of relations 88; of universals 117ff; principle of 90, 96ff; vacuous 95, 159

Accident 22, 158

ACKERMANN, Wilhelm 90n, 120n

Actuality 3f

Aggregate 114f. *See also* Class

Algebra: abstract 81; of classes 87, 92, 128; of numbers 18, 45; of relations 128

Alternation 84

Alternative denial 81f, 84, 94

Ambiguity 32, 58, 67

Analytical: geometry 81; philosophy 157

Analyticity 20, 22f; and existence 161, 163; and modality 143, 150–153, 156f; and postulation 35; and reductionism 41; and synonymy 27f, 31f, 151; contrasted with truth 130, 138; in artificial languages 32–37

Ancestor 115

Antinomy, *see* Contradiction, Paradox

ARISTOTLE 22, 81, 155f

Arithmetic 18f, 45, 81, 92f, 127f

Artificial language 32–37

Atomic sentence 23, 30, 166

Attribute 8–11, 18, 75, 108, 156ff; versus class 107f, 119, 122f, 153

Aussonderung 96

Axiom 35, 88ff, 96f, 100f; of infinity 89, 93; of reducibility 125n, 127

BARCAN, Ruth 156

Behaviorism 48

Being and nonbeing 1ff, 7. *See also* Existence

Belief 142, 144, 148

BENTHAM, Jeremy 39, 42

BERNAYS, Paul 15n, 90n, 97n

BERRY, G. G. 134

Biconditional 32, 84

Bind, *see* Bound

BLACK, Max 15n

BLOCH, Bernard 50n, 52n

BLOOMFIELD, Leonard 50n, 52n

BOOLE, George 87, 92

Bound, least upper 127

Bound variable 86f, 102ff; in ontological commitment 6, 12ff, 103, 108ff, 113, 128; in stratification 91n; erstwhile schematic 113f, 118f, 121–124; restricted to elements 97, 100; Greek 111. *See also* Quantification Variable

BROUWER, L. E. J. 14, 125n

BÜHLER, Karl 51

CANTOR, Georg 14, 92n, 121f, 126f, 129

CARNAP, Rudolf 14, 23ff, 45f, 158n; *Aufbau* 39ff; on modality 144n, 152–156; on semantical rules 33, 36; on synonymy 29n, 32

CASSIRER, Ernst 61

CHADWICK, J. A. 166

Change 65

Choice, axiom of 89

CHURCH, Alonzo 14, 104, 116; on modality 152ff, 156; on semantics 108, 132n, 135n, 142, 145n; his theorem 5, 96n

Classes: abstraction of 30, 76ff, 87, 94ff, 104, 159; abstractness of 114; algebra of 87, 92, 128; commitment to 45f, 113, 115, 122; determination of 89; existence of, in general 14, 18, 114ff, 125f; existence of, in special theories 39, 81, 90, 93–100, 113, 128; names of 30, 108, 113ff; positing of 71–77, 117–127; versus attributes 107, 122f, 157

Collection 114

Combinator 104f

Commitment, ontological 1ff, 8–11, 44f, 130f; to abstract entities 10f, 45, 73, 78; in logic and semantics 96, 112f, 116; in mathematics 13, 19, 103, 122, 127ff. *See also* Criterion, Hypostasis, Ontology

Common sense 45

Completeness 19, 89, 96, 116, 131, 137